Hi Linda,
Blessings to you!
I hope you will enjoy.
Nancy

ONE WOMAN, ONE GOD, AND A HORSE NAMED CJ

—A LOVE STORY

By Nancy Rose Blomiley

Copyright © 2013 Nancy Rose Blomiley.

All rights reserved. No part of this book may be used or reproduced by any means, graphic, electronic, or mechanical, including photocopying, recording, taping or by any information storage retrieval system without the written permission of the publisher except in the case of brief quotations embodied in critical articles and reviews.

WestBow Press books may be ordered through booksellers or by contacting:

WestBow Press
A Division of Thomas Nelson
1663 Liberty Drive
Bloomington, IN 47403
www.westbowpress.com
1-(866) 928-1240

Because of the dynamic nature of the Internet, any web addresses or links contained in this book may have changed since publication and may no longer be valid. The views expressed in this work are solely those of the author and do not necessarily reflect the views of the publisher, and the publisher hereby disclaims any responsibility for them.

Scripture taken from the King James Version of the Bible.

Scriptures taken from the Holy Bible, New International Version®, NIV®. Copyright © 1973, 1978, 1984, 2011 by Biblica, Inc.™ Used by permission of Zondervan. All rights reserved worldwide. www.zondervan.com The "NIV" and "New International Version" are trademarks registered in the United States Patent and Trademark Office by Biblica, Inc.™
All rights reserved.

Scripture taken from the Amplified Bible, Copyright © 1954, 1958, 1962, 1964, 1965, 1987 by The Lockman Foundation. Used by permission.

ISBN: 978-1-4497-9089-9 (sc)
ISBN: 978-1-4497-9091-2 (hc)
ISBN: 978-1-4497-9090-5 (e)

Library of Congress Control Number: 2013906207

Printed in the United States of America.

WestBow Press rev. date: 7/08/2013

ACKNOWLEDGEMENTS

To my Lord and Savior Jesus Christ:

I want to thank you, Lord, for bringing Jean C. into my life. We met through our Bible Study, and because we both are widows it gave us a special bonding time. Lord you led and we followed in a new friendship. She helped faithfully to bring my manuscript forth. Thank you Jean, truly a Jewel, in the Kingdom of God.

A thank you goes to my granddaughter Karlee. She helped to edit and gave to me words of encouragement I won't forget. You are an inspiration to my life. I love you so!

I want to give a huge thank you to my friend of so many years, Carol B. She has helped to bring my manuscript to completion. She gave me her knowledge and her love and that is one of many things that make's this book special!

Total gratitude and love goes to Collin my grandson in the pictures he took of CJ and me for the entire cover and those of CJ being the comedian he is. I am so proud and grateful of you Collin. You did an awesome job in editing the final draft of this book! I am confident the Lord will use your talent many times over!

A thank you to Tracy B. for sharing with me such important words of encouragement , when this book was yet a journal. To my long time friend Bette C. you are so special to my heart along with Cathy K. The three of us have been friends forever it seems and it was our wonderful Chinese Shar-Pei that brought us together. Thanks for all the encouraging words you both have given me. I truly can say that this book isn't just about my life! It is A True Love Story that involved many!

Table of Contents

Introduction		ix
Chapter 1	But God	1
Chapter 2	Childhood Dreams and Nightmares	7
Chapter 3	A Horse of My Own	11
Chapter 4	I was looking back to see if you were looking back at me	17
Chapter 5	Healing Came Under the Weeping Willow Tree	29
Chapter 6	Man Complies, God Provides	35
Chapter 7	Sudden Glory aka "ET"	47
Chapter 8	All Creatures great and Small, The Lord Loves them All	51
Chapter 9	An Unexpected Sorrow	61
Chapter 10	My "Fortune Cookie"	69

CHAPTER 11 AN ARTIST'S HEART	75
CHAPTER 12 FORGIVENESS IS MORE THAN A WORD	79
CHAPTER 13 PARTING AND RECONCILIATION	83
CHAPTER 14 CONFRONTING THE BIG "C"	87
CHAPTER 15 CJ BEY KINCADE	91
CHAPTER 16 A NEW ROLE FOR MY LIFE	101
CHAPTER 17 NEW LIFE	109
CHAPTER 18 REACHING OUT IN SONG	119
CHAPTER 19 FAITH AND "WUBBY WIPS"	121
CHAPTER 20 ONE MORE SPECIAL STORY	139

Introduction

WHAT IS GOD'S GRACE?

This is a true story about a woman and her family and how she sought God and found him. It's a testimony of how God's Grace can weave a beautiful tapestry out of so much brokenness.

It is about a relationship
and all that came with –
One Woman – One God
And a horse named C.J.
A Love Story

By Nancy Rose Blomiley

"This is the day the Lord has made,
let us rejoice and be glad in it!"
Psalm118:24 (NIV)

CHAPTER 1

BUT GOD

On July 26, 2006, I started to write about my journey through life. As I sit here, reflecting on all that has transpired during the years with my relationship with my Lord, I am in awe of how faithful He has been to me.

I was raised in a home where going to church was occasional. I was confirmed at age fourteen. As you came into the foyer of the church we attended, there was a large wooden framed picture of Jesus hanging on the wall. I never did understand that picture of Jesus standing on the outside of a big wooden door with his hand on the door latch, poised to knock on the door. Not until years later did the Lord show me in my heart what that picture represented. I wanted to know what it meant, but I was too shy to ask anyone.

It was at thirty-two years of age that God intervened in my life. I was angry and hurting emotionally. I was sitting on my bathroom floor shaking a fist up to the ceiling, crying out. "Is there truly a God? If you are real, where are you? Do you care about us as a family?" The "us" I referred to was my husband, five children, and me. I cried out, "God don't you care what happens to us? Our marriage is failing and I don't know who to turn to for help. Please, if you are real, hear my cry. Please, look into my heart. I want to be a good wife and mom! Why are things so wrong?"

> "Hear my voice when I call, O Lord; be merciful to me and answer me." Psalm 27:7 (NIV)

On that cold January evening, I can share with you how His love, like a soft warm fleece blanket, became totally wrapped around my very being. Through circumstances only God could arrange, I found myself being drawn by the Spirit of God to pick up the phone and to call a couple that I barely knew, basically to just say "hello." I knew them through my daughter, Christine. She had a friendship with their daughter. My reality at that time was thinking I am truly losing my grip. "Oh God, please, hear my heart. I am so scared, and I don't know what to do. I only know I can't go on the way I am."

I could believe there was a God, but the only teaching I knew was that of *"religion."* It was never about a *"relationship"*.

I didn't know my Lord and Savior. I only knew of Him, but little did I know that it was God who was moving me in a way that I couldn't understand at the time.

Feeling very desperate and at the same time very calm, I went to the phone book and looked up the couple's telephone number. I then went out to the barn to make the call that changed my life forever.

I went to use the barn phone because I didn't want my family to know I was hurting so bad and that I would go to this extreme. To talk with someone I barely knew? I only knew in my heart that I was at a breaking point and I was so very scared.

When Lynn answered the phone, I identified myself by telling her my name, and her response was, "Yes, Nancy, what can I do for you?" I really didn't know.

> "But God, So rich is He in His mercy"
> Eph 2:4 (AMP)

God was drawing me to a couple who were more than willing to help me to understand what it meant to have a personal relationship with our Lord. When Lynn and I finished our conversation, I was "maybe" going to their home, and I had told Lynn that if I didn't come, to please forgive me for this call. Shortly after my call to her, the two of them held the Bible and together they prayed for me. They prayed from the scripture:

> "Again, I tell you that if two of you on earth agree about anything you ask for, it will be done for you by my Father in heaven.
> For where two or three come together in my name there I am with them"Matt: 18: 19 (NIV)

I went to their home later that evening. I remember Carl talking to me about the fact that he believed I was a caring person. I was a good mom and a good wife. All I needed was *the key* for my life.

That key was Jesus Christ.

Carl and Lynn shared with me that they had received Christ into their hearts. They confessed to being sinners, they asked for forgiveness and then became the vessels that God could use to share the wonderful gospel of Christ with me and others. This is the purpose God has intended for each of us. The Lord has given gifts to all of us and Carl had a very special way of ministering to my heart.

The Lord brought laughter and joy to a woman who was broken by the world, and through Carl and Lynn, I heard the truth, and the truth set me free. I will be eternally grateful for their obedience. As I listened to them share, I made my decision. I felt in my heart I had tried everything to make things work. I remember thinking, "Why not? I've tried everything I know of already."

It was then that I asked the Lord Jesus Christ into my heart, and I asked Him to be my Savior and my Lord. I asked Him to forgive me for my sins and I surrendered my life over to the care of my God! I meant every word I spoke in the sinner's prayer. I didn't understand how or what would happen by making this decision, but I felt excitement in my spirit! In my heart, I received the Holy Spirit and the reassurance that I would spend eternity with Him. At the time of my death, I would be rejoicing with the angels because from this day forth, my name was written in the "Lamb's Book of Life". How awesome is it to know that you can spend eternity with the King of kings and Lord of lords? Scripture tells us:

> "Unless a man be born again, he cannot enter the Kingdom of God." John 3:3 (NIV)

We need to be "born again, spiritually". I tried all the time to be good. I wanted to please someone, mostly my human father, while I grew up. When I became a married woman, I wanted to please my husband, be a good wife and a good mom to our children. No one explained to me the real meaning of John 3:3. It meant that I needed to have my spiritual sight opened and my spiritual ears to listen. It's not about being "good enough". He accepts us as we are and invites us to come to Him with the heart of a child. I can have eternal life with Him at the time of my death. He will walk with me my entire life while I am on this earth and all I have to do is ask him to! Our Lord died so that we might have life.

> "He who has the Son has life. He who does not have the Son of God does not have life." I John 5:12 (NIV)

Don't you see? That's what the picture of Christ in front of the door was about for me. He is knocking on the door of every person's heart and it is up to us to invite Him in. It's just that simple. We, however, can make it so much more complicated.

> "Behold, I stand at the door and knock: if anyone hears and listens to and heeds my voice and opens the door, I will come into him and will eat with him, and he will eat with me." Rev 3:20 (AMP)

Maybe you never had anyone share with you the truth of the Bible, or maybe you did but you have fallen away from the truth. God has forgiveness waiting for each of us. All we have to do is ask Him. I was given a new sense of joy and hope which flooded my heart. Did my circumstances change all for the better? Absolutely! I now had hope for my family!

To surrender, according to Webster's dictionary, is to give up one's self into the power of another. It all started with me. The change began within my own heart. It does not mean to give up one's power to just anyone, but to understand that God is waiting for us to come and surrender to Him and Him alone. It is the best decision I ever made! Not once have I regretted asking Jesus to be my Lord and Savior because when you seek after the Lord, He will never let you down.

> "Seek (aim at and strive after) first of all, His kingdom and His righteousness (His way of doing and being right), and then all these things taken together will be given you be sides." Matt 6:33 (AMP)

As a young girl I was taught religion. I was never taught God's Word. I didn't understand the Bible and like a lot of people, the Bible I had sat on a shelf, and it regretfully collected dust. God's Word is a living thing! I had never been taught that it is in His Word we find the answers for our lives.

 # Chapter 2

Childhood Dreams and Nightmares

As a child growing up, I learned things like: "children are better seen than heard." You didn't question what Dad said. I lived in a very black and white type of thinking. It was all or nothing and I didn't ask for my way very often.

I did learn at a young age my animals were safe to love. They gave unconditional love. However, a pattern began to form in my childhood days, after losing my kitten to a tragic death, my Beagle pup to a sickness and finding my pet rabbit dead in the cage with an unknown cause. This all took place over a period of years. It seemed to me that it was my pet who would be the one to die. I came to believe I caused their death because I loved them. That of course, was a lie from Satan!

I mostly dreamed about horses at night. I needed an escape from the bad things that happened to me as a little girl which involved a brother who had his own set of problems. These bad things took the dreams I had of horses and gave nightmares to me instead.

I would wake up when I was around six years of age, as I recall, screaming. I remembered the cartoon faces that were suffocating me. It was awful to have those child friendly faces of Mickey Mouse, Donald Duck and other cartoon characters trying to suffocate me! They were supposed to be friends to kids. I now know it all had to do with a very scared little girl.

There were times my parents left me in the care of my oldest brother. It was during these times that he would wake me, tell me he would make popcorn and offered me soda, but in reality he wanted me to do things sexually with him that I didn't want any part of. I cried and cried and didn't want to listen to him!

I would go back to my bedroom. When I did fall back to sleep, I struggled with the balloon type faces that were going to hurt me. This happened several times more than I care to remember. As a little girl, I grew to have anger and hostility toward him. I wouldn't forgive him.

I don't remember when I told my mom but I thank God now that I was able to do so. I didn't want my oldest brother to be at home with me anymore when they went out. It was never discussed. The behavior stopped!

As I thought about my life, I did realize that somewhere in that time frame my brother went into the Naval Armed Forces. He was twelve years older than I so he would have been of age to do so. My parents obviously dealt with the problem, but I never knew what was said between them. It was never discussed, not even when I was old enough to discuss how I felt as a little girl.

As an adult I now understand how possibly talking to Mom could have influenced how I viewed myself for so many years. I needed to hear the words that said it wasn't anything I did wrong. I needed for someone to help me understand that I wasn't the cause! Without an adult correcting my information and helping me to understand differently, I grew up believing I was to blame in so many situations.

I know that I am not alone. We grow up having received messages that are distorted and often times it will then create a very low self-esteem. I am sure Mom thought it was all over and I would be okay as many parents might think. But, in reality, we become sad, angry, hurting people. I lived with a lot of false guilt and shame. As I grew up I didn't realize how these feelings were causing me to become someone other than who the Lord intended me to become.

> "For in you, O Lord, do I hope:, you will answer O Lord my God." Psalm 38:15 (AMP)

Chapter 3

A Horse of My Own

When I was fourteen-years-old, we moved to the lake. My parents purchased a house that was nothing but a shell. My Dad finished the inside. In the year 1954, I entered high school.

All I ever wanted as a young girl was a horse of my own. Instead of being boy crazy, I was horse crazy. The first horse I ever rode was a little black work horse named Daisy. I always felt I was born to ride! I learned how to ride her bareback. It taught me to have great balance. She didn't come with an instruction manual, but I rode her as if I had glue in my breeches!

The time came when I rode any horse that anyone would let me ride. I helped to show several horses for people who were trying to sell them. When I showed them to the customer, the horse was sold with a promised payment which I never received. Being an insecure young girl, what that said to me was, even though I knew in my heart I did a good job, I wasn't worth the payment. Again, I never received any support from Dad. Today, I have a better understanding of my Dad and how difficult his childhood was, however being a young girl at that time, I didn't understand why he treated the situation the way he did. It felt cold and empty to my heart.

During the first two years of high school, I helped to take

care of a young horse at the barn where Daisy lived. I fell in love with this tall sorrel gelding. I called him my Victory Boy.

I was asked to ride him, take care of him and do all the things necessary to make him into the fine young horse he became. This became a very special time in my life. I was so happy. I taught him tricks and rode him bareback wherever we would go. I wanted him to be my horse so much and even though he wasn't, this was the next best thing as I saw it.

We spent days and weeks and months together. I couldn't wait to get home from school each day and go to the barn. I would call him and he would come running to me from the pasture. Oh, the joy I would have in my heart as I would watch him running toward me!

Then without warning, the day came when the people who owned Victory Boy forbid me all riding privileges, and I was not to have anything to do with him. They had decided to sell him. I was so broken up. I thought I would never get over this. How could this be? Why was this happening?

The last time I saw him, I was walking home from church. From a distance, he began to call to me as he knew it was me. As we came close I asked his owner if I could say hello to him.

The man could not make eye contact with me but gave his consent. I put my arms around his neck and tears fell into his beautiful red mane. I told him how much I loved him because we were more than best friends and in my heart I felt if he was a part of me. When I was with him I felt he gave me that part of myself that was taken from me as a small child! I remember how I didn't want to let go of him.

However, his owner took hold of the reins and told me he had to move on, all the while he never once looked into my eyes. I wanted him to speak kind words so badly and to tell me he was so sorry this was happening in my life. I wanted him to tell me I could resume being with my sweet friend, but that was not going to happen. I never spent time with him again. I was heartbroken beyond description!

> " O Lord, the God who saves me, day and night I cry out before you. May my prayer come before you; turn your ear to my cry. For my soul is full of trouble and my life draws near the grave." Psalm 88:1-2-3 (NIV)

This scripture describes the pain in my heart. I was left standing by the roadside sobbing quietly. I was a fifteen year old girl holding my heart in my hands! I was so broken inside and the pain seemed almost unbearable! I couldn't understand what I had done to deserve this, and no one would tell me. I walked home, crying every step of the way.

I felt so alone, unloved and unworthy! As time went by, I found out that the girl, who kept her horse at the same barn, had spoken to the owner's wife. I was aware that she had been spending time at their home and I wondered why she was doing so. When I confronted her, this girl admitted to telling lies about me to the wife. She was jealous of me because of how I was able to teach both her horse and this young colt I loved so very much, different tricks. Jealousy had broken my heart!

The owner had come to my house and told me I no longer could have horse privileges. He just stood outside the screen door and told me with his head bowed and his eyes staring at the ground. When I questioned him why, he turned, slowly shaking his head as he walked out. Later, I found out what had happened and received a confession of guilt from the girl, and I unleashed my fury toward her. I would have done the same to my father but we were raised to know you didn't challenge Dad or even question him. My hopes and dreams were smashed. My heart was totally crushed!

Have you ever been blamed for something you didn't do? I think of people who have been put in prison for some crime they didn't commit. I think of the great people of the Bible who were in prison for spreading the Gospel, but most of all,

I think about our Lord Jesus. He was falsely accused and He paid the ultimate price for each of us. He does hear our hearts cry!

> "Answer me when I call to you, O my righteous God. Give me relief from my distress; be merciful to me and hear my prayer." Psalm 4:1, (NIV)

My parents once again didn't do anything in my behalf. Instead, Dad told me I had no business taking care of someone's horse that wasn't mine, and what did I expect? I couldn't understand how a man who rode horses a great deal of his life could not understand my love for horses! When I was a young girl he told me stories of his favorite horse, a little Buckskin mare. Her name was Daisy also. He told me everything that he trained her to do. I have loved animals all of my life!

God has helped me to understand about the unconditional love that He created within our pets. Not having had a healthy relationship with my human father, it has been through my love for the animals that I learned how to receive the unconditional love from God, my heavenly Father.

This young horse was a living expression of God's love and He played an important role in my life! I am so grateful to the Lord for the love I shared with him. His memory will always be sweet in my mind and heart. As a young gal I wasn't taught about the Gospel of Jesus Christ, so for years I was in bondage to pain and unspoken anger. I truly believe the Lord carried me through the hurtful years. He was always there! I just didn't know it.

The years that followed were both happy and troubled for me as I began to date. I was drawn to the man who lived on a farm, and of course he had a horse. I rode his mare Coco often, and as usual I enjoyed horse back riding so very much. I felt as though the horse and I were one as we went across the fields. It was the only time I felt free of the pain I held within my heart. I eventually became engaged to this man.

Coco was very much a joy in my life at this time. There came a day I rode her about three miles from the farm to a friend's house. The friend and I sat and talked and when it came time to leave she offered to ride part of the way with me. As I turned Coco to leave, she suddenly began to stumble and fell down and landed onto her side.

It all happened within minutes and my left leg was pinned under her weight. I called to her to get up as the pain in my leg was extreme! She tried several times and finally lifted herself enough for me to be free. However, in trying to get my leg free, I twisted and turned my leg over and over again. Only when she was able to lift up a little, my leg came free.

Later in life, I would learn from my chiropractor about the twisting of my tibia-bone and how it affected me. Mom had to cut my pant leg on my jeans to get them off. My leg had become so very swollen. I didn't know what was happening to my Coco but the end result was she died on the spot. Just like that! I was told later she had an enlarged heart and had a heart attack. To add salt to the wounded heart, I had my boyfriend's father say to me, after he had been drinking, "you're the girl who killed my horse." Things really fell apart for me at that time, and I shut down emotionally hoping the pain would leave.

It wasn't long before I broke off the engagement but not because of Coco dying. I found out my fiancée was unfaithful to me. He didn't show up for our date. He had accused another man of doing something, which gave him an excuse for himself. In reality it was because he was with another girl and figured I'd never know different. I accepted his lame excuse until the next day when I came face to face with the man being accused. I had met this person briefly at our drugstore earlier in the week.

Jerry was his name, and I confronted him about his behavior. He totally denied ever having seen my so called boyfriend and proved to me he was telling the truth! I then learned I had been lied to and made a fool of.

> "Hear, O Lord, my righteous plea; listen to my cry, Give ear to my prayer- it does not rise from deceitful lips, May my vindication come from you, may your eyes see what is right."
> Psalm 17 1-2 (NIV)

Chapter 4

I WAS LOOKING BACK TO SEE IF YOU WERE LOOKING BACK AT ME

A short time later Jerry and I connected again and as we shared with one another, there was a wonderful attraction and romance was in the air. We eventually began dating and about six months later, we married. Was it a rebound from the first man or was it a way of getting out of my parents home? No doubt.

However, I was also attracted to the sharp dressing, good looking young man who stole my heart! His big brown eyes and great smile proved to be more than my heart could withstand. I was nothing more than a young girl, with much insecurity looking for my knight in shining armor. Did he own a horse by chance? Afraid not!

Having met him briefly at our local drugstore, during the time I was engaged, I was sitting at the fountain having a soda. He noticed my hand and made mention of my engagement ring. He asked me if I was serious about that, pointing to the ring. My reply was,"yes I am. " When I left the drugstore, he already had left and had gotten into his car.

As I crossed the street, he came around the corner in front of me, and I looked at him as I was about to cross the street. He looked at me and continued to look at me, and I looked back at him until I thought, watch where you're driving!

There is a silly old country song that describes the whole scene. Some of the lyrics are:

I was looking back to see if you were looking back to see, if I was looking back to see, if you were looking back at me! You were cute as you could be just standing looking back at me, and it was plain to see I'd enjoy your company.

It was pretty funny at the time! It was exactly what the words of the song described. It brought much laughter in later years. We were staring at one another for so long I really did wonder if he was going to hit another car.

Perhaps this was a divine meeting for our lives, and God would begin to orchestra a life long journey with Jerry and I. Scripture warns against marrying an unbeliever but in our case, we both had not met Christ as our Savior.

Our wedding took place on November 7, 1959 in the Lutheran church in our town. It was a small wedding. I would have liked to have had more, such as a long dress with a beautiful train. I would have had a big dance hall rented so we could have danced the night away. I could not express that to anyone. I didn't know how to ask and I wasn't asked what I would like.

Jerry and I at our wedding

As I have reflected over the years, I wondered to myself if he saw some things about himself in my husband and didn't like what he saw. They were alike in many ways. There wasn't any communicating between Dad and myself. I was too afraid of him by then and felt rejection most of the time. I never felt my Dad's approval of anything I did in my life so why would that change now?

Three months after being married I became pregnant with our first baby girl. I had a hard delivery and the emotional state of mind I was in was awful. It was because of my husband drinking during this time, and the drive up to the hospital with him was putting me on an emotional roller coaster. There were so many times I wondered why I didn't run from the relationship at that time. I always came up with the same answer. I had no one to run to.

When, at last, my baby girl was born, I looked at her and fell in love. She was so tiny and precious. I was so afraid of doing something wrong, and yet I knew in my heart of hearts that I could be a good mom to her. She became the focus of my attention, and I loved her so.

My Mom did support me during this time and she helped me

on more than one occasion to realize that I would be able to take good care and love this tiny person. She weighed six pounds and eleven ounces, and that felt very tiny in my hands. I was, however, a very proud mom. We gave her the name of Cindy Lee.

Our sweet baby girl, Cindy

A peaceful life requires a peaceful mind. My cartoon childhood nightmares did stop. However, somewhere in the first years of marriage, I began dreaming again, and these dreams were nightmares also. They consisted of large bears trying to get into our home, and I was the only thing that stood between them and my children. You know how dreams can cause you to break out into a cold sweat? The dreams were horrifying to me, and I woke crying on the evenings when my husband was out drinking.

In my heart years later, I believe that God showed me that my husband had a drinking problem, and there was much turmoil happening in our marriage. The bears represented the alcohol and the behavior that goes with it. "It" was trying to consume our family. The first thirteen years of our marriage were filled with turmoil, anger and sadness because of the alcohol. However, during these years, my husband did do something special for me that helped to heal a broken part of my heart. He bought me a Palomino gelding whose name was Rebel. He was a very gentle horse and didn't have any vices. I had many wonderful rides on him, and it helped because I would always love horses and now I had one of my own.

In an attempt to shield myself from the pain I felt when I lost my best friend, years earlier, I shut off the kind of deep love I once had felt for the young chestnut gelding. He had filled the great hunger for love that I never received from my human father. I was never hugged or told that I was loved. I understand how years ago many people lived with the pain I lived with, including my Dad. He also had a very painful childhood.

Years went by and Reb became sick. In those days there wasn't any real cure for his disease. The time came when he was put to sleep. Once again, I believed that any animal who I loved would die because of me loving it. This had become a self-fulfilling prophecy. For years, it haunted me. The turmoil within my soul grew daily. Would I ever believe there was a God in heaven who loved me?

> "The Lord is close to the brokenhearted and saves those who are crushed in spirit. A righteous man may have many troubles, but the Lord delivers him from them all." Psalm 34:18 (NIV)

There was a time after our first daughter was born that we had not been going to church. Occasionally we would go as a couple. However, one evening the young minister came to our apartment and asked why we weren't coming to church. What do you say to that question? We gave answers like, working two jobs, and I was busy with our baby but we knew in our hearts it wasn't the best answer.

At that given moment the minister stood up, walked to the apartment door, swung it open with force and banged it against the television set. In an angry voice he said, "Well, you can either come to church or go to hell and be damned!" After he left, we sat there stunned, looking at one another. Jerry said to me, "You know what you can do with your minister, don't you?" That was the beginning of a lot of heartbreak. How different our lives may have been if that young minister would have been able to nurture us and help us to come into a relationship with our wonderful Lord, and His mighty word the Bible. It was not yet to be.

Our first four children were born very close in age, with Cindy and John being less than a year apart. Then two years later another daughter, Connie, was born, and then another two years our daughter, Christine was born. Lastly, six years later, our youngest daughter Jody was born. When the fourth baby was born I remember being so exhausted both physically and mentally. I'm sure my hormones were very unbalanced at that time. I don't remember going to a doctor to even talk about how exhausted I was. I can look back and wonder if that is where I became hypothyroid, and years later I would suffer because of it.

**Front row: Jody, Nancy, Connie, Christine
Back Row: John, Cindy, Jerry**

I loved my family very much and I wanted to be the best I could be, but in reality, I felt wounded, alone and very tired. Jerry and I didn't have the communication skills required for a healthy relationship. He worked during the week and drank both Friday and Saturday on most weekends. He played cards with his friends until wee hours in the morning. On Sunday, he recovered so he could work on Monday.

He came into the marriage with a lot of baggage as I did. I was alone a lot of the time with our kids and felt emotionally abandoned by him. Sadly I didn't have a relationship with the Lord Jesus. In the lonely times, I tried talking with my mom, and she did her best. When I was a kid, she always tried to be the go between with Dad and me. She would talk with him and then come back and tell me the results. However, Dad had a different attitude after I became married. "You made your bed. Lie in it." He didn't want me talking with my mom because it upset her.

I had no one to turn too for guidance. It was then the Lord in his Mercy, reached down on that cold January evening as I sat on the bathroom floor crying out, 'God are You real? Is there a God?' He ever so gently put his arms around me and helped me to turn to him.

My cry was heard by my Lord.

> "When you get to the end of your rope, reach out and touch the hem of His garment".

The world teaches we must be strong and help ourselves to be in control and to not show weakness. We must take charge of ours lives and make the best out of what we have, but the Lord has a different plan for us. As we seek his face, seek his word for answers, we then can receive from the Lord everything he has for us. Healing of our emotions will take time, and it certainly has in my life.

Depression has often times tried to keep me in its ugly grip, and it bites at my heels. It is only by the power of the Holy Spirit that I come to the cross time and time again. His love is always there waiting to embrace me with His answers.

When I reflect on the past, a lot of what I experienced was not something I would have chosen. When I look at what I did with all the years of the past, I can only say that, for the most part, I loved my husband despite all of the short comings. I loved my kids so very much. They were the reasons for decisions I made.

More than anything, I didn't want them growing up in a broken home. I always felt in my heart that I wanted to give to them more than what I had. As I reflect on the past, I feel today we had some great things that families don't necessarily have today.

We had our animals and chores but also times of laughter together. We had memory making events shared as a whole family. We had a shared dinner time together that is unknown to a lot of families now-a-days. That is so important!

It may not seem a big thing, but it was. If the drinking days could have been removed with all of the ugliness that it brought to my life, my children's lives and my husband's life, this story would be told differently today. I realized my husband carried a lot of pain in his own heart. His own father said things to him that hurt him deeply and should never have been said by anyone, especially a father to a son.

I witnessed his father saying this awful thing to him in front of several people. I know this contributed to his drinking. The things said were plain ugly. My husband never had anyone to nurture him or help him become all that God wanted for him! My heart grieved for him.

I also realized I married a man much like my Dad. I couldn't fix his pain. The childhood pain of not feeling love from my Dad just snowballed into my marriage. I came to understand that in many ways my husband and I were very much of the same fabric.

There was never an excuse for the painful behavior we experienced because of the drinking. Our kids could have friends over during the day but never for a sleep over on the weekends because of the drinking. Those years were hard on us all because the drinking always ended with it getting out of control and the Jekyll and Hyde personality would rise up. The message I received was the same as in the past. You know in your heart that it isn't true. I was predisposed to this message due to the amount of years I heard it from my Dad and now again from my husband. It was my fault. I remember trying ever so hard to keep things together, and I would strive harder to be a better wife and mother.

We did a lot of simple things like sledding in the winter and building snowmen for each member of the family. When the snow was deep, the kids would make igloos and if you listened, you could hear them laughing inside the house they built. I remember never having enough dry mittens. Fun was what you did with your sisters and brother and cousins. I would do a lot of baking. One of the favorites, potato pancakes, was something I would make especially when our niece Peggy came. I smile now as I write this. She loved them so. We had memories to hold in our hearts.

We always had time to make hot fried donuts dipped in sugar. We canned dill pickles and tomatoes and froze bags and bags of sweet corn. All of this we did together.

There came the time when we made the investment of buying a snowmobile, and we rode many places as a couple.

Back then, husband and wife rode together on one machine. It was beautiful to ride trails in the Kettle Moraine forest and enjoy the beauty of the snow and friendships. The kids had a lot of fun on it also, and I will never forget our son, John, driving it in the pasture. He was not all that big but he drove it around, after Dad had instructed him, carefully pulling the girls on their saucers.

We got along better when he didn't drink, and I rationalized the problem for years because he only drank on weekends. He only drank beer. I would say things like, "He only drinks beer and he holds a job." Not until I went for counseling, did I come to understand the dynamics of living with alcoholism. It's not how much you drink necessarily it's what you become when you drink. He was not a person who could drink just one beer. It would always lead to an entire day or into the wee hours of the next morning.

So many times I came home from a special occasion, such as a birthday party, alone with the kids. After putting them to bed, I would be alone waiting for him to come home.

There is role playing that each person gets caught up in. When an alcoholic counselor described the personality of each of our children, such as a hero, scapegoat, lost child or clown, I was so stunned. It totally described my children's personalities.

It was devastating to me to learn how one person's addiction not only affects them, but all who are involved. I was very co-dependent. When the counselor asked me how I enabled my husband to drink, I'll probably never forget what I thought, "Enable? My goodness, I do believe enable means to help someone." As I looked into his eyes, I thought, "You fool!"

There is no way I would help him to drink knowing all the consequences we had suffered. However, there were things I did that enabled him and later learned what they were.

I may have reached out for help sooner had I understood what I was living in and how I was affected along with our children. Many women would have left this marriage. I will admit there were times when I wanted to more than anything, but I had no where to go. Parents whom I believed wouldn't help me. There was no sister or brother to help me. No God to my knowledge who cared about me.

My second brother was the closest person to me when we were kids. He was taken from my life tragically in a car accident when he was twenty seven. I was twenty one. He was the only person I remember looking out for me and he displayed anger many times at my oldest brother and his behavior. I grieved terribly over his death. My dad became very bitter over his death and blamed God for taking his fishing partner. He was filled with grief and anger and didn't know how to deal with his loss.

I also have a sister six years younger than I. We were never close and to this day we don't have a relationship. That is sad for both of us. I would have liked having her in my life but I know now I wasn't the only one in my original family that was capable of holding grudges. Once again I was accused of doing something that never happened. I am sure that if Christ wouldn't have intervened in my life the way He has, I very easily would have become someone who lived with bitterness as a constant companion. Never learning about forgiveness would have sealed my fate! Again I say "Thanks be to God"

I always wanted my Dad's approval. I wanted to know that he loved me. I just wanted to hear those words. The Lord knows what is in our hearts. He knows what is best for us. He is always there to help show us the way through the pain and not around it.

As hard as some things have been in my life, I would like to think I chose to walk through the pain with the Lord. It was in the forgiveness of all of the people who had hurt me deeply as a child, but especially my Dad. I began to understand what inner healing was all about. It is the inner man that so often needs to be healed. It requires you to have a heart that is willing to look at yourself, deep down in the very core of your being. Do you remember? All we have to do is ask! Not too long ago, I heard this said, and I am so grateful to God that I have learned how to forgive.

Not forgiving someone is like taking a teaspoon of poison every day while you are waiting for that person to die. How sad is that? I lived for many years hurting, resenting, unforgiving, not understanding my pain. It truly took being set free. I know there are many people who feel the same and don't understand why their lives are so broken and empty.

Forgiveness for me is a constant companion. I can't live even one day with peace or joy if I am not prepared to forgive. This includes forgiveness toward me. I realized sometime ago that I am the most critical of me, and I need to be kind to myself. Not in a prideful way, but I need to give myself a soft place to land when I do make a mistake.

The story I share in Chapter five has taught me how God can use anything He wants to in order to help us in our journey. I will never look at a willow tree again without remembering this great lesson.

Chapter 5

Healing Came Under the Weeping Willow Tree

God helped me in a very special way. It all happened during a time I stood under the willow tree that my Dad originally had given me as a little starter branch. He told me how to put it in water until roots were visible on the end of this branch. Then as it received the new roots, I could find a place to plant it, and it would grow into a strong willow tree. I had been cutting the grass, and as I came to where the willow tree now was standing, I noticed all the dead twigs on the ground and I began picking them up.

Some were large branches and others were smaller but as I picked them up, I began to feel a deep sadness in my spirit. I prayed out loud and asked the Holy Spirit, "What is this I am feeling?" Immediately the Lord gave me a vision of all kinds of clutter in my life represented by the dead twigs and branches. He helped me to see that my life was being cluttered with unforgiveness, resentment, and a lot of negative thinking that would eventually become bitterness, if not addressed.

Tears began to flow down my cheeks. I cleaned all the broken branches and twigs up and as I stood under the tree, it was like being under a huge umbrella. The sun light came streaming through the branches, and I felt love coming down to me from my Father in Heaven. I couldn't stop weeping. There were cars that would drive by, and I worried that someone I knew would stop. I thought to myself, oh, how foolish I would look.

Nevertheless, it felt as though my heart was being cleansed. Nothing could take away from the Lord's healing touch that was so important for my life in Christ. When I looked up into the main branches and saw a lot of little branches growing out of the trunk of the tree, the thought came to me that these were "sucker branches." They were draining the tree of strength and good health.

In my vision, I saw myself being drained of energy in the same way because of those awful things I had been hiding in my heart toward people who had hurt me deeply! Without having any kind of tree pruning experience, I began to cut out all the sucker branches. As I did this, I gave to the Lord memories, one at a time. The deep seeded hurt and unforgiveness. All of the resentments I held against family members and others were in those memories. The painful memories of my Dad for never being the kind of father I so needed as a little girl and the feelings of rejection I had received from him.

I needed desperately to forgive him. Finally after much time and tears, I said out loud, "Dad, I forgive you. I do forgive you," all the while I was still crying and snipping the small branches off. I had a lot of pain in my heart.

God helped me to see that forgiveness is a decision and not a feeling. I didn't have to feel like forgiving; I had to choose to forgive him. "Forgiveness is giving up the desire to punish the person who hurt you." Those words spoke volumes to my heart then and to this day. When I had finished, I looked up into the huge umbrella of the Weeping Willow tree, it no longer looked cluttered. It was clean, strong and beautiful. Praise flowed from my heart. I gave all of the glory to my Father in Heaven! He had set me free!

> "So if the son sets you free, you will be free indeed!" John 8: 36(NIV)

Oh how we need to cry out to Jesus. He offers so much hope! I am so grateful that I was a Christian at the time of my Dad's death. I know in my heart that I tried to take the message of Christ to him and only God knows what he heard and received. He didn't talk about it. One of the things he did speak of was how angry he was that God took the only fishing partner he had. Like so many, he blamed God for my brother's death. My Dad died suddenly of a heart attack on Christmas Eve, 1976.

Mom called us after we had spent time with them for Christmas and had gone home. I can never explain how God brought healing between us that evening, but there was a time when just he and I were in the kitchen. I'll never forget how he spoke to me. It felt as though we were friends. I was very much aware of his smile and the warmth I felt from him.

Forgiving him made a huge difference in my life! God does know what is in our hearts at all times. I truly understand why the Lord in His goodness allowed me to learn what it means to forgive. I know that it is not our nature to forgive the pain of someone hurting us and people do take unforgiveness with them to their grave. We pay an extremely high price if we don't learn how to forgive. It can be in our physical health, emotional, or mentally. It can and will change who we are. God provides His truth for our lives and with the truth comes healing! Experiencing God's healing love can and will change our lives for the better if we trust in Him.

A few years after Dad's death, Mom was diagnosed with

breast cancer. One day she showed me a mass on the upper portion of her breast; the size of an orange. It was weeping and she covered it with gauze. It was awful. I promised myself and my daughters from that day forth that I would have regular mammograms and never put them through what I went through with her.

I took care of Mom through the twenty five radiation treatments. I didn't receive any help from my sister or brother. I was angry with them and some of their responses I received from them broke my heart. I felt Mom deserved to be cared for by all of us. This was our Mother!

One day Mom asked me to make an appointment for her with a lawyer. I had no knowledge of why and even though I asked, she just said she needed to talk to him. On the way to that appointment, she said these words to me. "Nancy I don't know what I should do about your sister." She was so sad, but in my heart I knew I needed to be still. All I replied was "Mom, that's between you and her."

My Mother, before she became ill, went to live with my sister. Mom wasn't happy and one morning called me at about 5:30 a.m. asking me if it was alright if she came out to my home. Of course, I said, and wanted to know if she wanted me to come and get her. She said, no, she would drive out.

When she arrived she disclosed she wanted to move back home, to the town she had lived in for so long. I had five children and much going on in my life so I didn't discuss with Mom the reasons for her departure other than she did say she wasn't happy there. I just wanted to help her however I could. We helped Mom to move out to a senior citizen apartment. I knew after my Dad's death Mom was very sad and her heart was broken. No one can fill that emptiness except the Lord Jesus and I am glad she had a relationship with Him.

I would put my arms around her and hug her. She seemed so small in my arms. Jerry and I and our children tried to be her support system and I know in my heart, we tried to do the very best we could. We all loved her so very much!

After Mom went into the hospital for a mastectomy, she told me one day that as she lay in the hospital bed, she closed her eyes and saw the hands of Jesus reaching out for her. She knew He was telling her she could come to Him, but she said, "no Lord not yet, I need to get my house in order."

She told me later, how very beautiful His hands were. She just couldn't get over how beautiful they looked. All she could see were His hands and part of His white gown covering His arms. Tears filled my eyes when she told me this. It was so beautiful to think of how His presence filled her room.

One of the things Mom loved to do was to listen to a little cassette of mine that had songs on it that I sang. They were songs that I believe the Lord blessed my life with, by giving me the gift of writing songs. These were songs that God gave to me to encourage me at a time I needed encouragement.

September 27, 1980 would have been their fiftieth wedding anniversary, Mom died on that day. It was so hard to say "Goodbye for now Mom." I knew she went home to be with our Lord Jesus but my heart felt so much grief. Over a period of time, the Lord helped me to believe and to receive from Him the knowledge that His purpose for the songs was not only to build my faith, but to minister to others. All He wanted from me was a "willing heart to do so". For a time, I put all thoughts of this on the back burner in order to care for Mom.

Only my Father in Heaven could know the depth of grief I felt and He was there with me. It was a hard time for us all. God worked His peace into our hearts and when the time came, I dedicated my album to both Mom and Dad.

My album cover

CHAPTER 6

MAN COMPLIES, GOD PROVIDES

In a near by town a new Christian recording studio had just opened. The Lord put into action the birth of my album that was entitled "Jesus, Lord and King". There was never a doubt that this was orchestrated by the Lord. After the album was completed the studio moved. (It was the only album to my knowledge produced there.) It came for a divine appointment and then it was gone. It moved to a much farther location and one of which I more than likely wouldn't have wanted to travel too. God made it all come together.

I could complete this album and still care for my family. The song Jesus, Lord and King was my victory song about the journey of my life and still is! "Jesus, You are Lord and King, Jesus, You are everything, Jesus gave new life to me, More abundantly, Praise His name."

We all need to get to know Him in a very real relationship, one in which we walk and talk daily with Him. One in which we learn to read and study His word, the Bible, and to learn of Him and become more like Him.

As we prepared the songs, Mark who was producing the album shared what was on his heart about the song. "Love

Living Me" I have prayed about this song and I believe the words tell of your life, where you have been and where you are now in your walk with the Lord and the last is yet to be seen. We both agreed that it needed to be a three part song. And so it was.

Each song is filled with memories for me. They speak of what I was praying for, or what I had been working through in my life or maybe it was taking time with my Lord, hearing from Him. One song in particular, "Try the Lord" was my prayer for our son. I prayed so much that each of my family members would come into a relationship with the Lord. The album was an accomplishment in my life and I feel honored to have done it. I trust that the people who hear the songs will receive from the Lord blessings and healing that only God can bring to them.

Today, I can look at the cards I kept from people. The words of the songs ministered to them. Often, it was right where they were in life and God gave encouragement to them. They would send me a thank you card and share with me how the words of the songs ministered to their hearts at a particular time of their life.

The greatest commission we have been given by Christ is to share with others about having a real relationship with our God. That will always be a strong desire of mine. I believe we need to rely on the Holy Spirit and He will lead, if we will listen for Him.

His leading, gave me an opportunity to share with someone very dear to my heart. She was my babysitter for years. She had been raised in the church all of her life, and only as God could arrange we went horseback riding one time together and while we rode, I talked, she cried, I talked, and she cried more. There were moments for me when I would think to myself, "Be quiet Nancy!"

So I would stop talking and somehow it just continued to be one of those special times with God. I talked, she cried. I shared with her the love I now had in my heart for Jesus. I said, "Mary, it's not about religion, but rather a relationship with our Lord"

I don't remember exactly how many days had gone by when she came and told me what this all meant to her.

She said no one had ever talked about the Lord the way I did. I was so excited about my relationship with Him. She could see the joy in my face and when I shared how she could have this same joy, it would cause her to cry. She felt like she had missed so much in the years she attended church. God had a plan. Her heart was open to Him She told me she asked Christ to be her Savior and Lord. I was so filled with joy! There is nothing more fulfilling in life for me than to help someone understand what a relationship with God is about.

Praise You Lord for my sweet Mary and her willingness in learning that she could have a personal relationship with You, Lord. You are so very awesome and I won't ever forget that day horseback riding with her.

It was in 1972 that I had accepted Christ and shortly after that my husband quit drinking. I came to the place where I said to him in love, I can't go on like this, we need to get help, it has to be either me and the kids or the drinking but not both. There were times I had threatened divorce, wanting him to stop, but this time was different. I had the peace of Christ in my heart and I knew I had to stand firm. I was scared, but felt the strength of my Lord walking with me. We made a decision to go for counseling. Our life slowly began to change for the better.

> "But those who wait on the Lord Shall renew their strength; They shall mount up with wings like eagles, They shall run and not be weary, They shall walk and not faint." Isaiah 40:31 (NKJ)

I began to trust in him to come home on the weekends and that was a huge thing in itself. There was more laughter and happiness in all of our lives. I no longer had the nightmare dreams ever again! We became part of Living Waters Fellowship. I will always be grateful for Karen and Jack and the love they shared. In their home they provided some of the greatest teachers of the Bible.

Many wonderful loving people embraced us and we remained a part of this great place for over ten years. It was truly a gift from our Lord for us to be a part of them. We had developed good friendships in Christ. My friend Ruth took so much time in helping me to believe in myself. God knew the brokenness of my heart and He gave me a friend who stood beside me. To this day I am so grateful for the gift of her friendship. The Lord gave her insight and wisdom. Ruth and Ron became good friends to us. We both loved them so and had good times and much laughter throughout the years.

My friend Mary taught me about the destructive behavior alcohol brings to a family and what I needed to learn about myself. What being co-dependant meant. Growing in Christ causes you to stretch. There are new choices to make.

God provided a way, when there didn't seem to be a way. One summer He provided our family the opportunity to buy a swimming pool. It was a twenty eight foot pool. We earned the money by selling strawberries out of our garden. It was a little patch. The normal route that people took going to their homes had a detour that summer. Instead they had to go right past our home. This opened a door of opportunity we wouldn't have had.

One evening as we all sat down to eat our dinner I wanted to say the prayer. I asked the Lord to help us to earn the money for this pool that a friend was going to sell. I remember so clearly asking the Lord for five hundred dollars to help make up the difference of our tax return that we were short of but willing to use for the family. I heard some snickers about what I had asked. It just didn't seem like this patch of strawberries could bring us any kind of income of that size.

The patch had grown all together, so it was not easy to pick the berries with out stepping on plants. In reality it was a very small patch. We couldn't believe the abundance! People came from all over, when they heard about our berries. We picked more strawberries that season then we could keep up with. It was so outstanding! God blessed and blessed and blessed! We all worked so hard together, doing all the things necessary to provide the berries for people.

Jerry would take berries down to the airport and sell them with the kids on Father's Day. I stayed at home with a couple of the girls and sold berries out of the garage. We set up a large table and had quart boxes of large juicy berries that made your mouth water just to look at them. It was an awesome sight! We had given God our best effort!

The life of the berries was short. We had to work hard and fast. The fruit of our labor was awesome and we were able to provide a wonderful source of enjoyment for our family for many years to come, as we earned well over one thousand dollars toward the beautiful pool. God was so good to us! It proved to all of us that if you give God your best, He will give you His best…You can never out give our Father! We were all so happy and grateful. It was a wonderful time in all of our lives. We worked together as a family with the goal of bringing enjoyment to all of us.

The well deserved swimming pool.

Our pool gave us wonderful hours of fun and enjoyment. We had many good memories. Even though we couldn't take those vacations, we had hours of bonding right out in our pool and later we would share a meal together. Many wonderful memories were made during this time in our lives.

When the kids were smaller they had ponies and later as they got older, horses. My girls and granddaughters to this day love and ride horses and have their own. Our little farm consisted of seven acres of land, and every bit of it was filled with projects and animals.

We decided to get a milking cow. And so we did! Then there was the great idea of milking goats, because they were smaller and easier to handle and so we did just that. We learned how to handle the milk very carefully and milked in a stainless steel milk can. We would put it into our freezer quickly to cool and we all drank raw whole goat's milk which is very healthy for you.

We also had a fun time teaching our good friend Dick about the taste of goat's milk. We loved Patti and Dick and their family so very much. One day at a picnic we wanted to see if we could fool Dick and have him drink our goat's milk without him knowing it. We were pretty confident. Patti and I smuggled the milk into the refrigerator without Dick seeing it as he was late in getting home and was the last person to sit down and eat his dinner. In this process, Patti served him a glass of milk as she conversed with him about his day. He had drunk over half the glass of milk and Patti and I were hardly able to contain our laughter. Dick asked Jerry what was going on with the wives and Jerry gave him this response, "Gosh Dick, I don't know, unless it's because you just drank over half a glass of goat's milk." Dick always said out loud, you'll never get me to drink that stuff, UGH!!!! We laughed so hard that day. It was so funny. Dick had to confess that we fooled him good. He never would have known. He said "The taste of the milk was great".

The first goat we purchased was called Freckles. She was of the Saanen Breed, all white in color. We had gone to a farm in which they raised goats and milked them. They were involved in showing their goats and they were one of the largest farms that produced goat milk for marketing. Here we learned that a registered goat could have a tattoo in the ear.

Well you guessed it! When we got home the kids ran out to the barn to see if our Freckles had a tattoo in her ear. Sure enough, she did! That meant that we could possibly follow up and get her papers and her off spring could be registered.

We became involved for years in showing our milking goats. The kids loved it and had fun with other kids who were involved. Our son John loved to crawl into the pen with the baby goats. He would curl up with them all snuggled around him.

I took a picture of this as he had fallen asleep with all the babies around him and as I write, I can see the picture on my kitchen wall. It does make me smile. We had many adventures and lots of Blue ribbons and even a Grand Champion. Each of our children learned the value of caring for their animals and taking pride in how clean they looked and how good of a job they could do in the show ring.

We went to the National Goat Congress in Iowa and hauled a small trailer behind our Toyota station wagon with goats and children inside the trailer, mind you. I shudder when I think of the possibilities of something bad happening.

The kids loved it and begged to ride in the trailer and the highways weren't like they are now but even still! They will tell you all about that adventure. I believe God has His angels watching over us, even when we don't make good decisions at times "ARE WE THERE YET?"

When we arrived in Iowa, we went to the huge barn, where hundreds of goats were in their pens. We set up our pens for our goats and had an extra one that we used to sleep in. Oh my! Can you picture this? There were hundreds of goats that never stopped voicing their objections to being there? All day and all night! There wasn't one moment of silence! NOT ONE!

Now for my husband, who could sleep through most everything, it wasn't a problem, but to Mrs. B. it was a different story. I remember lying awake and counting the Baa's. It was pretty funny and you had to be there I think to really appreciate this motel filled with live animals. It had also begun to rain and we had jackets on and I began to feel the continual drip, drip, drip, on my jacket. So in the middle of the night we had to move to a dry spot. What an adventure for the Huckleberry Finn Family!

The kids of course thought it was fun! When they showed their goats, they were dressed in white shirts and white pants and white tennis shoes and looked VERY sharp! They had embroidered emblems on the back of each of their shirts that said SUNNY DELL DAIRY GOATS, which my mom had embroidered. We pinned them to the back of the shirts. It was so cool! They did an excellent job of showing animals!

Chores taught them work ethics that so many people lack in our world today. Before the goats could be taken into the show ring, they were clipped and bathed and had their feet trimmed. Each of our children had the responsibility of helping and that was a contributing factor to the success we attained in the years we were involved with these wonderful animals.

When we no longer were showing goats, we were showing horses, and each weekend we would be hauling someone to a horse show. You could always count on dad to be standing at a spot on the rail with the big camcorder sitting on his shoulder as we just had to get those rides on tape. Such joy! The girls can tell you many funny stories about those years. We always tried to make a good thing happen, even if we didn't have expensive horses or brand new clothing and gear.

We made memories! Wonderful, great memories! We laugh about those things to this day. I remember how we would go to a horse clothing sale and find wonderful bargains. At one sale I remember Christine finding a brand new pair of riding boots to wear showing her horse, and was excited about them because they were five dollars. She insisted on buying them! However, they were two sizes too big!! That didn't stop us from buying them and sticking balls of cotton in the toes of the boots. We do laugh about that still today.

Connie, Chris, and Jody were each actively showing a horse. Connie and Chris showed in saddle seat classes and Jody showed in hunt seat classes. The very first family horse we ever had was enjoyed by our daughter Cindy. She was an Arabian Mare named Aka. She came with a foal by her side and was bred back. Cindy did a lot of riding on her and it was wonderful. Horses were so much apart of our lives then and still are.

Because of having the animals we didn't take yearly vacations to different places. We did however try to bring fun and laughter to our family in doing things that involved each of us. When I look at how my children were raised, I don't have regrets for teaching them to be responsible for the care of the animals or for working together as a family unit.

I have stood at many ringsides over the years and watched people. The attitudes I have witnessed in both the children and adults are sad at times. If the value of a blue ribbon becomes more important than being courteous to someone next to you, or having a good sportsmanship attitude, I truly believe we have lost something really important in life. We all can struggle from time to time with our attitudes but when it becomes a way of living, it then becomes very destructive.

I believe my family did our very best with all of our animals, putting their needs first before our own, knowing they were dependant on us for their care. I am very proud as a parent for the way my children understood that and gave of themselves. They worked hard, and they learned that you don't always get a reward each time you put effort into something. Eventually the hard work and perseverance gave them the big blue ribbon, along with the satisfaction that they all had done a great job.

When we weren't showing goats, we were showing horses.

Chapter 7

Sudden Glory aka "ET"

His registered name was "Sudden Glory". In 1982, an Arabian horse of Egyptian descent was born. He was a bay in color, which can be a deep red color with black tail and mane. He had four white socks and a white star on his forehead. Two years later, in 1984, he became my companion. The dream of owning this beautiful boy was more than my heart could conceive.

As I waited for him to grow up another year, I spent time getting to know him. Taking care of him and just appreciating the fact that he was mine. When the time was right he received training. When I saw him for the first time, he was being shown at the Wisconsin State Fair Park in halter classes. I fell in love with him. I will never forget how I felt when he was delivered to our home. He had those four white socks and a white star shape on his forehead. He was a beautiful Bay Gelding. He was so beautiful! I remember walking alongside of him, feeling like I was the groomsman to this beautiful horse. How privileged was I?

The joy and love I had experienced as a child was back! His registered name was "Sudden Glory" but his call name was ET. His sire's name was "Glorybound." How perfect was that! ET had a very gentle personality. When the girls had horses, it was ET who became the low man in the pecking order. I would get angry with him because he didn't defend himself the way I thought he should.

One day the thought came to me how Jesus never defended himself. It really spoke to my heart and I found myself thinking about why He didn't. Really think about it. Do you know the answer? If Jesus was who He said He was, then He could have called a legend of angels forth. My heart tells me this; He was willing to do his Father's will. It was all about doing his Father's will.

In the following years I rode my "ET" out on the trails. I remember, going out on the trail and singing and rejoicing with my beautiful horse. It truly became therapy for me! It was my time with God and the gift He had given to me.

The Lord always had a way of using my animals in my life to teach me about himself. God makes himself known to us in so many ways. I am so blessed to have come to know Him with the heart of a child. He continues to speak to His children today through the power of His Holy Spirit. I have learned how to listen and to walk in the direction He is leading. I have learned how to speak to Him from my heart and then to sit quietly and listen for His voice.

My Sudden Glory horse.

CHAPTER 8

ALL CREATURES GREAT AND SMALL, THE LORD LOVES THEM ALL

"My sheep listen to my voice; I know them, and they follow me." John 10:27 (NIV Bible)

In this story, I share how I believe God still speaks to us today. He speaks to us through His divine word the Bible and I cherish His word in my heart. As I wrote in my journals years ago I would pray about those things that were upon my heart. God would answer me and I would write down what I believed came from Him. I trusted Him. He encouraged me and carried me as only my Father in heaven could do. It is according to His will that He gives us His answers.

> "Morning by Morning, O Lord, you hear my voice; morning by morning I lay my requests before you and wait in expectation." Psalm 5:3

This took place the week of April twenty ninth, 1984. I wrote about this day back then and as I was journaling now I found it tucked away in a photo album and I decided to include it as I know the Lord would like for others to be blessed in the way I was. It was a week in which we had learned of three different friends who died suddenly of heart attacks.

As I made my way out to the barn that morning, I was very heavy hearted. As I approached the open barn door, my eyes fell upon the small body of a kitten. I stopped and picked it up. It was cold and lifeless and I laid it on the riding lawn mower. It was a little tiger striped kitten. My heart overflowed with grief. Tears ran down my cheeks. I watched our cat Ziggy, as she made her way to the shaving barrel and as she disappeared into the barrel, I had to go and see. Perhaps she had others that were alive. My heart yearned to see a new life. I walked over to the barrel and lifted the feed bags. There lying by her mother's side was a little black kitten, also cold to the touch and lifeless.

I reluctantly took the second kitten and laid it beside the first one on the seat of the lawn mower. I felt a tremendous amount of sorrow and I cried out to the Lord. I had spent precious time with my Lord early that morning and it felt in my heart as though His presence had never left me. I walked from stall to stall feeding our horses. The two kittens had been lying on the seat of the riding mower for a long time now but as I finished the last horse, these words came to mind.

"Take this lifeless kitten, place it in your hands and blow warm air on it."

My response to hearing those words at first was, "Well I'm glad I'm here alone in the barn. If someone was watching me, they might think I had totally lost my mind!" However, these words were very strongly impressed upon my heart and mind so I did just that. I picked up the first kitten and brushed off the dirt and hay. I cupped the lifeless body in my hand and began gently blowing my warm breath over the very tiny head. After what seemed a very long time I saw one of the tiny paws give a little wiggle.

Having had animals of one kind or another most of my life and seeing death have its way in the lives of some of them, I thought it was a reflex. Then as I stood, convinced it was no more than that but continuing to pray, I saw the back leg give a small but convincing move. My heart began to pound rapidly. I scarcely could believe what I was watching take place. I decided to take the kitten to the house where I would find the heating pad and put the little body on something really warm. About half way to the house, I stopped in my tracks when the thought came to me that I should take the other kitten along.

I sure had a hard time with that! I somehow could accept taking the first kitten to the house but when I thought about taking the second one, I spoke out loud to the Lord, "But Lord this kitten's tongue is actually extended out of the side of its mouth". The Lord then spoke to my heart and I pray that I will never forget these words:

"Things don't always look as they really are. Right now this kitten looks dead, but then so did the first. What will it hurt if you just follow what you believe in your heart is from me?"

So I did! I took both little kittens and hurried to the house! There I wrapped them in a warm cloth and began searching desperately for my heating pad, which I couldn't seem to find! I was getting frantic!

The Lord brought my attention to a large patch of sunlight that was flowing from the window in my bedroom and across my bed. I felt compelled to kneel down next to the bed, and as I did, the Lord once again spoke to my heart and mind:

> *"Now lay the kittens in the Son's light,
> and they shall receive life."*

It wasn't long before I saw a miracle of miracles! Both kittens were moving. I watched the tiny chests move up and down. The sounds of two hungry babies soon brought a joy to my heart that was indescribable!

In a short time I decided they needed their Mom. I wondered if Ziggy would accept her new babies after all this time and under these conditions. At first, I was afraid to give them to her in fear she would lay on them and perhaps injure them, as she was a first time mom. I prayed over them and I believed in my heart that the Lord would protect them, as HE was the one who gave them new life.

When I got out to the barn Ziggy was still in the barrel. I gently took the two kittens and laid them on her tummy holding my breath as I did. The kittens began wiggling around on her and she looked up at me as if to say," Thanks mom, for all your help." She settled down and began purring loudly. I knew all was well. I began to Praise the Lord for His goodness and mercy!

Later I went back out to the barn to check on her and as I looked into the barrel there were four little heads bobbing around. It was a sight that brought tears of overwhelming joy! The Lord taught me an important lesson through the lives of these kittens. Jesus died, but He rose from the dead and we also will be raised from the dead if we believe and receive our Lord Jesus Christ as our Savior and Lord. He blessed me so much that day, by allowing me to witness what I know was a miracle! What a powerful God He is! He gives to all of us new life every day as we allow Him to transform us by the power of the Holy Spirit. I knew these two kittens were cold to the touch. I knew they were dead. They had been lying lifeless for some time; before I listened to the Lord speak to my heart, and then follow what I believed in my heart came from Him. I knew God had brought New Life, where there was death! I sat down and wept with a heart full of gratitude.

I am thankful today that I kept this story as a continual reminder of how great our God is! My kittens received new life! In my heart it felt as though the Lord gave me New Life when my ET became my horse. The brokenness I felt as a young girl was now being coated with a salve of healing ointment each time I rode him. Horse back riding once again became therapy! I know in my heart that because of the pain I went through as a small child, I didn't want to trust anyone. I am grateful that I loved animals and still do with a great passion. The message I carried in my heart during the years of growing up was a lie and I needed to acknowledge that!

> "You can't change something
> you don't acknowledge."

The Lord created us with feelings. Anger, sadness, gladness, hurt and shame. Up to that point in life the only real feeling I could identify was anger. Once I was able to understand and acknowledge that whatever may have happened that caused me to feel anger, the first reaction or feeling I may have had most likely was having hurt feelings, but because I didn't acknowledge the hurt and deal with those feelings, it then turned into anger. The person I was the angriest with of course was me, because I thought everything was my fault! Learning, how to let go and let God is a life process.

In the years ahead, I had decided to learn how to become a dog groomer and have my own business. I knew I loved dogs and helping them to look good was something I came to enjoy.

I couldn't believe you could get paid for something you totally enjoyed doing. Jer and I remodeled what was our little milk parlor and I became a self-taught groomer for many years. I had a friend who was a groomer and she shared important tips which helped me to do a great job.

I took pride in having the dogs I groomed look just as beautiful as possible and loving animals made this a wonderful job. Many memories were made which include the people. Some became very good friends. Marc and Carol are still my loving kind friends and I truly am so blessed to have them in my life. Nancy's TLC is still operating today, but with a new name and owner, my daughter Christine. It is now TLC Pet Grooming by Christine.

As the years went by and the kids grew older many stories could be told. However, each of our children eventually married and because I didn't want the empty nest syndrome to settle in, I became interested in showing dogs. Once again, I believe it was one of those GOD incidents.

My niece Kim had shared that there was a dog show being held not too far from my home. I decided to go and watch. It was a Specialty, which means it was of one particular breed, the Chinese Shar-Pei breed. I believe God allowed me to fall in love with this breed of dog. He wanted me to learn how to keep laughter in my life on a regular basis and I sure can testify to the amount they have brought.

I chose the brush coat Shar-Pei. There are two types of show quality Shar-Pei. The horse coat and the brush coat. There is a third coat, but it is pet quality called the bear coat.

There are so many memories that were very funny. There was one in which I had driven to the store and was coming down the isle very slowly seeking a place to park my van.

My big male Shar-Pei, Frankie sat in the passenger seat and he and I were watching this man as he was walking straight toward us. His whole demeanor said he wasn't paying attention. His shoulders were slumped. His head lowered and he was looking at the ground. I watched him coming closer to the front of my vehicle. He was oblivious to the vehicle coming at him.

I had almost come to a complete stop, when he looked up and his face seemed so very sad. He first looked at me in the driver's seat and then over to my wonderful passenger.

Here sat my wonderful funny looking dog with huge wrinkles on his face and body. Frankie just watched intently and the man looked at him face to face and gave out with the biggest smile and for several moments we just smiled. We then gave one another a thumb's up. As I watched him walk away I saw his shoulders straighten and I could tell he just seemed to feel better. Can you see all the little ways God touches our lives? Even in a smile!

Now I have to tell you about my very first Shar-Pei who was named Creamy Chin Hogg. She was born in 1986. Creamy was her name, Chin was her Mom's name and JD Hogg was her Dad. I gave her that name because that was my way of remembering the lineage she came from. The picture that makes me laugh the most of course is the picture of her sitting on the hill. Her reaction to me calling her was so funny because she knew I was calling her but decided to ignore me. It was very hard for me to not laugh and I truly believe she knew what a comedian she was!

Never having had a Shar-Pei, this girl taught me many things about patience. She always had a way of finding out whether or not I meant what I said. She could be sitting outside enjoying the warm sunshine and I would come and open the door and call her name to come in.

Most of the time I would be in a hurry and she would lift her nose to the air sniffing the breeze , all the while she had her eyes on me but wasn't getting up to come into the house. It was only when I took the first step outside the door, called her by her full name, "Creamy Chin Hogg!" I would then get her attention. She would get up off her little behind and while wagging her tail, she would promptly come into the house, looking up at me with this attitude of, "Hi Mom! I was only kidding you!"

At other times when she became a mom herself, I watched her love her babies and care for them deeply. She would crack me up with laughter when my grandchildren would come.

Creamy just had to smell their little ears. We would laugh at her as it would tickle their ears and she loved doing it!

She loved my daughter Jody very much. When I had purchased Cream at the age of six months, she almost immediately bonded to Jody, to the point of growling at me when I had come into Jody's bedroom while Cream was lying on her bed. As I approached my newly purchased prize she let out a growl. I didn't know this came with the package! The only chance I had of sharing this girl with Jody came because Jody was gone to school. This gave me time to work with this little "Boogie Butt" for the show ring. This breed now has been a part of my life for the past twenty six years.

I can't tell you how many times I have thanked the Lord for this. They are great teachers. They are quick to forgive, they give unconditional love, deeply devoted to their family and will claim you at any opportunity they can! Cream had two litters in her lifetime. In the second litter a little fawn colored female pup was born. I named her Suzie, better known as Too-Z, I didn't intend to keep Suzie but it was Christine, who said to me, "Mom she is a winner". Because she favored Suzie

I did keep her. In everything I accomplished with my dogs, my heart was filled with gratitude to God and all that He helped me to attain.

> "I can do all things through Him who strengthens me." Phil 4:13 (NIV)

Before the Chinese Shar-Pei became part of the American Kennel Club, I had one last opportunity to champion Suzie as part of the Chinese Shar -Pei club of America. It came on the last day of being able to show. The Chinese Shar Pei Stud book records would be turned over to the American Kennel Club the following week. How is that for God's perfect timing? It was awesome! More tears of gratitude!

Dog Patches Creamy Chin Hogg and her puppies

Creamy Chin Hogg

Mom, are you calling me?

Ookie and Cookie,

Magoo, Taco, Suzie and Ruby

The "One and Only"

Chapter 9

An Unexpected Sorrow

In 1988, our daughter Christine was married and she and her husband Bob were going on their honeymoon when tragedy struck. While on their honeymoon, Bob died! He had gone into the ocean to swim as so many others were doing. A short time later a swimmer noticed him floating face down and went to his aid. How could any of us see God in the midst of all of this; in each step of all that Chris had to live through?

It changed our lives forever, but especially for Christine! I also have to admit that it was the closest I have come to seriously questioning my faith. I couldn't understand! God was a God of Mercy? Then how could this horrible time be upon us? For Bob to die during the time he was on his honeymoon? A month after where the wedding dance was held, we all stood across the street at the funeral home? The only emotion I was in touch with was ANGER! I remember how very angry I felt—it just was so unfair!

Coming home one evening, I was driving our truck and it was pouring rain and I was alone. I was expressing my anger to the Lord and searching for an answer from Him. I began to cry. It made it difficult to see the road. I pulled over and stopped on the shoulder of the road. There I pounded my fist on the steering wheel, crying out. I sat there crying and feeling so bad for my daughter. The rain coming down on the truck windows expressed the solitude of the moment.

I knew God was listening. He always hears what is in our heart. As I sat for a time listening to the rain, I felt His peace. I told the Lord I would just wait on Him to help us all, to help me in the unbelief I was feeling, to restore my faith and love for Him, and that right now wasn't where I wanted it to be.

I felt the wind had been knocked out of me and for a long time, I waited and watched and listened for God to speak to my heart and through His Word.

I prayed constantly for our daughter. He proved to her over and over that He was with her every step of the way. The pain was in describable; however God gave her strength when nothing else could!

"Time heals all" is not the truth. As we work through the pain, what ever the circumstances and allow God to be the great healer that He is, we then can move on in our lives in a healthy way. The Lord was with us in our time of need and I praise Him so much that my daughter knew Him and loved Him during this period of her life. He was there for her to lean on, over and over again. He ministered to her so much. I pray in time my daughter will share with those who need to hear this testimony of God's unfailing love. There is a part of Chris's story that I truly would like to share.

We had moved Christine back home with us. Once again, I had no clue what God had prepared for me. One of the hardest things for me as a Mom to accept was the fact that I wasn't with my daughter in her time of need. We were so far apart. She was in a foreign country. Not being able to put my arms around her. How very awful that was! Words really can't express the depth of pain our hearts were dealing with!

During this period of time I had made contact with Mary Ellen, the editor of The Orient Express Magazine. This was our Chinese Shar-Pei magazine. She expressed to me that in the next issue of the magazine she was looking for articles on "How our dogs can help us during the grief process." Little did she know what our family was going through. I told her how this tragedy had come upon us. She asked me if I would write an article about this and I said, "I will have to think on it." I really didn't want to write anything. I didn't want to relive the pain once again and be thinking about how my daughter's dreams had been so destroyed! It actually took three calls from her with the last one saying, she needed an answer because she had a deadline.

At this time in my life, I had four wonderful pups that were around six weeks old. Chris would hold them and love on them with me. One day in particular I was in the kitchen. Chris was in the doorway and said quietly to me, "Mom, come here." I walked over to her and she pointed to the male pup. He was sitting by himself and Chris said to me "Doesn't he look like Mr. Magoo, Mom?" We both stared at him and watched as his sisters were playing with one another and he just sat on the sidelines watching and his expression was priceless! Both Chris and I looked at him and then at one another and broke out laughing. We laughed and laughed until we both cried and hugged one another. It was the first time we had felt anything but sorrow.

Needless to say, this little boy was given the name of Mr. Magoo. And I surely hope that those who read this, remembering the cartoon character Mr. Magoo, will smile. When he went to his new owner she kept this name for him. As I described earlier, I planned to sell all of the pups, but Chris insisted that the little fawn colored female puppy was going to be a winner!

Money never determined what I did with my puppies and even though I could have sold her to a couple. I chose to not do so. This puppy was special. I have already shared with you that it was my Suzie, better known as TooZ. The puppies brought the laughter Chris and I experienced that day with Mr. Magoo and we realized there would be more and it helped us to understand the scripture

> "Because of the Lord's great love we are not consumed, for His compassions never fail. They are new every morning; great is your faithfulness." Lamentations 3:22- 25 (NIV)

I did write the article about the tragedy that happened with Chris and Bob and I submitted the article for the magazine. When I received my magazine, my article had been printed. Weeks later I received a letter in the mail. The return address read British Columbia, Canada. I began reading the letter inside the envelope as I walked from the mail box to the barn, where Jerry was working. It was from a woman who lived in British Columbia, Canada and raised Chinese Shar-Pei. I read the following:

"Nancy, I think our lives have crossed paths."

She began telling me about how she and her husband were on a vacation in Puerto Val-larta, Mexico. They were on the beach at the time of this awful tragedy. Now she was as shocked as I when she read the article in the Chinese Shar-Pei magazine. What are the chances of this happening? She and I shared the same breed of dogs.

You will have to understand a very important part of this. The Chinese Shar-Pei was almost extinct not too long before this time. The breed was making a come back and here were two women, one from Canada and one from Wisconsin who before this happened never met in any way! Only God knew how to make things happen so we would get to know one another! To this day we keep in touch with one another. I truly believe with all my heart that God wanted this for us and so he arranged it totally. When I walked into the barn and read the letter to Jerry, he got goose bumps. It was hot outside and he didn't have a shirt on. He was just as much in shock as I was!

God is so faithful to his children! I will praise Him for the blessings He brings to us. No matter where we are, He is there also! This became a story that was not only how God gave us healing through this beautiful litter of puppies, It was also doing what God placed in my heart through the calls from Mary Ellen. Being obedient once again to the nudges He gave me in her calls. I truly believe God wanted me to write this article for the magazine. It was the key to bringing our lives together. Our lives were touched by God in so many ways!

The Lord renewed my faith in Him. Even though I myself couldn't be there God was! I came to understand that God our Father provided for Chris and in doing so, one of the things he provided was a woman who is a mom and who would try to help. Joan's heart went out to Christine. Joan and I have emailed one another over the years. A couple of weeks ago we both talked about this tragedy by e-mail and I would like to include what she e-mailed me. Please remember this happened in 1988. It is now 2011. It is now twenty three years later. Her recall of all of what she witnessed is unbelievable. She wrote:

"I think it is wonderful that you are writing a journal and I think the way we were brought together was the hand of God. What are the chances that a Shar-Pei breeder would be at the exact spot and time of another Shar-Pei breeder's tragedy, and in another country? I had no idea until I read your story that we were connected. I could hardly believe what I was reading! I remember your daughter so vividly even after all this time. Poor sweet girl was alone in a foreign country, on her honeymoon, with her new husband dying right before her eyes!

I just had to try and comfort her. To calm her, I kept telling her, to tell him to breathe. That was her job. She seemed to calm down some as she had a very important job to do and needed her wits about her. (what Joan didn't know about Chris was that she worked as a Vet. Tech. for several years and had training in staying calm and concentrating on the work at hand.) One doctor came forward; he was from Montreal, giving Bob mouth to mouth resuscitation. When he became exhausted, the doctor from New York came to their aid and tried to help. The ambulance came and we wondered what the outcome was, but never knew until I read your story in the Chinese Shar-Pei Magazine."

In reality this is only a portion of the entire story. There are so many things that happened, such as the van which they called an "ambulance" ran out of gas on the way to the hospital. When Christine told us all that had happened, all of the devastating things that contributed to the death of her young husband, it seemed the darkness would never leave us.

It wasn't until that particular day when Chris called my name and asked me to come and see the puppies. Then I could honestly say the darkness began to leave. We stood and watched and laughed until we cried! But it was a good cry that day! God used many things, including a Chinese Shar-Pei litter of puppies. Healing love came to us over and over. My daughter's heart slowly began to heal.

Suzie became the first AKC championed Chinese Shar-Pei in the State of Wisconsin, "Champion Glory bound Chin Son Suzie." In the following years what Chris had said about Suzie being a winner proved to be true. Her accomplishments included being championed twice in the conformation ring. The first was with the Chinese Shar-Pei Club of America and the other with the American Kennel Club. I also put a CD Companion Dog Title on her in obedience. I was so very proud of her.

We also did CGC titles (Canine Good Citizenship). As years came and passed, I always loved the challenge of trying to better myself and what I could accomplish. I went from putting Conformation Championships on my dogs to showing in obedience and also learning how to teach dog agility for people who just wanted to have fun with their companion. Dog showing was another way of learning how to be someone who could persevere. I accomplished five Championships and was so thrilled!

My dog and I walked the path of the fifteen point Championship without having a professional handler doing it. It just didn't happen over night, but became a journey of learning to have patience and perseverance. This is the way God builds His character in us.

FIRST AKC CHINESE SHAR-PEI CHAMPION IN THE STATE OF WISCONSIN

Doubled Ch. Chin Son Suzie-

Wisconsin's first A.K.C. Chinese Shar-Pei Champion, Glorybound Chin Son Suzie

Chapter 10

My "Fortune Cookie"

One exceptional story was that of my "Cookie". Cookie was one of two puppies born to Creamy Chin's first litter. She was a cream in color and had a beautiful show quality body. I was showing her and had points accumulated toward her championship when an accident took her out of competition. She and my husband's rottweiler, Greta, were playing and as they passed one another, Gretta grabbed Cookie's rear leg and the cruciate ligament in the knee was torn.

My heart sank. All of my dreams to have this beautiful girl become a champion dissolved right there in the horror of what now was inevitable. She would have surgery on the leg. I was devastated! She already had 7 points toward her Championship. My focus became that of taking care of her and making sure that she received the best care I could give her. The leg atrophied and it looked as though there wasn't anything left but skin and bone. At that point in time, I felt our show days were over. I needed to trust God in this situation. To believe He held a plan for me and Cookie.

"And be constantly renewed in the spirit of your mind (Having a fresh and spiritual attitude)."
Eph. 4:23 (AMP)

I would lay hands on Cookie as the Bible instructs us to do and I prayed for the healing of her leg. When she became well enough, I decided to swim her in a stock tank we had. I would put warm water in it and the tank was deep enough for her to swim in place. I smiled often as I held my girl in place as she swam, and just the soft sound of click, click, click, as her toenails slightly touching the bottom of the tank could be heard. Cookie loved the water. She didn't struggle with me at all. Normally the Shar-Pei I have had didn't like water. Cookie did! I have been blessed to see the hand of God in situations like this.

I remained persistent in doing everything I could to bring my girl back to wholeness. Wholeness was my goal, and after some time and lots of hard work I felt I could continue to show her, but this time it would be in obedience. It was my understanding that because she had a scar on her leg that indicated a surgery she no longer could be shown in conformation where she had accumulated her points. Some time later, my friend Cathy and I were at a show, when out of the blue, a professional handler walked up to me and asked if she was "finished", meaning, "did she have her Conformation Championship?" I replied, no and the reason why. It was then he said for me to get her back into the ring because he saw the potential in Cookie.

He also said that the scar came from an accident and not from a genetic correction. She is beautiful and deserves a Championship. Driving home from the dog show that day, I told Cathy that I really was thinking about going after her AKC Championship in Conformation. She told me to go for it. This wasn't a genetic fault. This was an accident and so I began another wonderful journey.

I gave thanks to God. We definitely had worked hard to have this opportunity. There was a Chinese Shar-Pei Specialty in Minnesota a couple weeks from then and we were going!

The big prize would be a five point major! There were a lot of professional handlers at this show. I was a breeder handler, and felt the professional handlers who did this for a living, could do so much better than I could ever do. I believe with all my heart that out of the blue, this professional handler, sent by God came and helped me to receive the reward that God planned ahead of time.

> "Now to Him who is able to do immeasurably more than all we ask or imagine, according to His power that is at work within us." Eph. 3:20 (NIV)

I proudly showed her and tried my very best. As we stood waiting for the judge my heart was pounding so hard! As he came toward me I held my breath! He handed the winners ribbon to me and said, more than anything "I really liked her movement!" Do you know how sweet to my ears those words were? I cried like a baby with gratitude that day! My girl was only three points away from her fifteen point Championship. She needed her second major. She completed this a few weeks later, with a four point major. Perseverance, perseverance, and more perseverance! The Lord had given me a fighting spirit. He wouldn't let me give up! Thank You, Jesus! Remember how in the beginning of my show career with my dogs, I said that someone once told me to hang in there, especially if you place in the ribbons? Most often in dog showing, Champions are made in a year, sometimes less, sometimes longer.

I didn't have a lot of dogs to choose from if I wanted to continue in the conformation show ring. Losing my Cookie at the time I did, when she had accumulated seven points, was a huge heart break without a doubt. What needed to happen for my Cookie girl was big! She needed both her major points. In order for there to be a major given at a show, there has to be a certain amount of dogs participating. That sometimes was difficult to do. The breed wasn't that popular and the numbers were down in participants. A major can be a three, four or five point major. In reality she needed both of her majors to become a Champion! Both majors are earned under two different judges.

When I made the decision of putting her back in the ring, I did this with a child like faith. I believed in my heart that the Lord would walk with me. I felt because of what that handler had said to me earlier, I did have a good chance at getting her Championship. Even though Shar-Pei that were crème in color didn't always win. They weren't as popular as the fawn color or the red fawn with a black mask. The rest of this testimony is history. Cookie became an AKC Champion at the ripe old age of three. The last points she took was the five point major and a couple weeks later a four point major. She ended her conformation career with sixteen points. From the very beginning to the completion of her Championship God was so faithful. We also did Canine Good Citizen titles. In Obedience, they became Companion Dog titles. It was a challenge, and yet it was a great time in my life.

God always dealt with me when I needed to take a look at my attitude. He helped me to examine my heart and ask the question of "Why are you doing this?" I originally felt that dog showing was to be something that I did with my companion dog to have lots of fun.

My relationship with my Lord kept me having fun because He kept me being honest with myself and Him. Gratitude is another great tribute to God. He taught me how to have a grateful heart! The memories of the dog showing days are too numerous to write about. Over ten years of learning all the things that either could make me a better Christian, a better person or doing it for all the wrong reasons. I am writing this to help others understand how keeping the Lord in your day every day gives you the opportunity constantly to choose to walk in His Way or that of the world. Did I do this perfectly? By no means!

I believe one of the greatest blessings in my life at that time, was to work toward Cookie's Championship. It required of me a lot of hard work and determination. When the judge handed me her wonderful ribbon and said to me, "I loved her movement," tears began to flow remembering all the hard struggles she and I had gone through. Despite all of the hard work, she and I were now standing in the winners circle.

We don't always see what is ahead of us in this life's journey, but keeping our eyes on God does bring victories. I can't find the words to describe the joy or the gratitude I have in my heart. Success does come for many in the world, but eventually without Christ in our lives; the success will become hollow and empty. The valuable lessons I learn as a Christian are priceless! When you set goals, and learn to persevere no matter what you come up against, God will bless your efforts and commitment. This is my testimony to His faithfulness!

Champion Glorybound Fortune Cookie

My beautiful champion, Glory Bound Fortune Cookie

CHAPTER 11

AN ARTIST'S HEART

In the years I showed my dogs, I also got the idea to sculpture a Shar-Pei statue. It just seemed to me, there wasn't any out there of nice quality, (Of course that was my opinion).The sculpting I saw, were statues with big ears. The Shar-Pei have inverted "tulip petal "looking ears. So, I thought about getting some clay and just seeing what I could do. Talk about child-like faith.

I prayed and ask the Lord to help me. I knew God gave me the talent but I didn't have any experience in how to sculpt anything! I look back and see a woman who was willing to try, and try I did. In my first attempt, I created a life size adult Chinese Shar-Pei statue. Jerry and I made them out of cement and people loved them. Oh yes, they only weighed in at about sixty five pounds a piece. No little project for me! WOW!

In doing this project, one of the lessons I had to learn was how to take constructive criticism from my husband. It was hard to sit and sculpt the clay this way and that way and to work for hours on one part, only to have hubby come in and look and when I asked what he thought, he would reply with something that at first I thought was very critical. Oh Boy!!!

It was hard to receive this at first, having grown up with feelings of not being good enough or doing things well enough.

I felt I never did anything of value in my Dad's eyes. I needed to be able to receive criticism from my husband. It took spending time with the Lord and asking him to help me realize the comments Jerry made about them, were actually correct. I needed to change something in my sculpting, so I got rid of my attitude and opened my heart to the possibility that he was right.

The greatest joy for me was not just the people loving them, but at different shows, I would be at a table with my statues selling them. The dogs and owners would come out of the showroom and the dogs would literally pull their owners over to where I was sitting. They would jump up and put their front paws on the table in order that they might sniff this new dog, thinking, "Who is this new pup on the block?"

One woman ordered a statue and asked me to paint it the color of her dog. So I did. When she received the statue, she placed it in her home in a room she wanted it to be in. She had put her live Shar-Pei in another room before doing this. After she placed the statue she let the dog come in to see the statue. Immediately the dog went to the ears of the statue and after sniffing that area she went to the butt!

I laughed so hard when I looked at the series of pictures she had sent me. I have always believed in my heart that God brought a lot of laughter to people through this wonderful breed of dogs! I know we have laughed many times over the silly things our dogs do and maybe it is another lesson for us to realize, what an awesome God we have. He laughed and played when He walked on this earth. Why did the children run to Him?

Maybe we as adults need to run to Him, not just when we come to the end of everything that's wrong, but in each new day giving thanks and asking Him to help us to find His peace and joy.

Love = A Rottie

The Real Deal

A Mother's Love

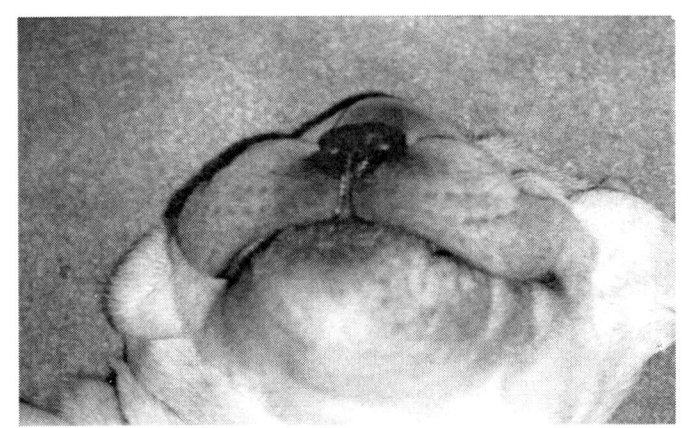

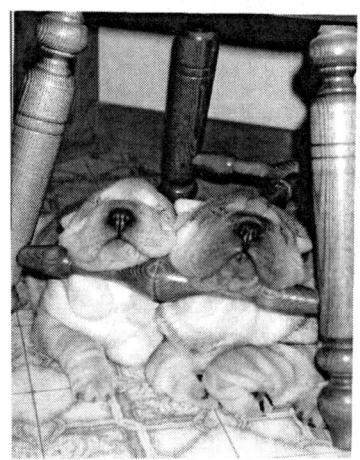

Chapter 12

Forgiveness is More Than A Word

In the year 1998 Jerry retired. I know that for some men, retirement can be hard. It became that for us. Because of the inner turmoil that some men go through, drinking became an issue once again. We had over twenty five years of Jerry being sober. To those who deal with a spouse drinking, learn the difference between real sobriety and what the counselors referred to as a dry drunk. Sobriety comes with surrender. I believe it is surrendering our will over to the care of God and getting help with the problems that caused the person to drink in the first place. It is my opinion that unless that happens, people who stop drinking simply put a cork in the bottle.

It is by that person's sole determination and will power to not drink and not one of surrender. Many people go for years without drinking. When I was in alcoholic counseling, for co-dependency, my counselor once said to me that Jerry would go back to drinking some day. I didn't believe him.

Forgiving was something I learned from God. Back when the children were young, I was so grateful that the drinking had stopped. I truly swept away a lot of what needed to be talked out. The word "sorry" wasn't in my husband's vocabulary very often. Finding closure for many things that had been said in anger didn't happen for me. The verbal abuse had made a footprint on my heart. I could no longer live with him after I found out he had gone back to drinking.

Another chapter in our life was about to take place. I believe my hubby was depressed after retirement and the demons he fought were many. Do I believe God walked with us during this time? Absolutely! I know in my heart God began working in both of our hearts during this time of separation.

In the year 2000, a home up north was purchased, we split finances and he went to live in his world of retirement while I stayed behind. I faced having to split our six acres and to try and see if I could build a small retirement home on the three acres I would have. The vision I shared with him as we looked out over the Kettle Moraine under the huge oak tree was that of a small retirement home, nestled between the two hills. It would not leave my heart.

At one point in time, we had gone up north together before I realized he had gone back to drinking. I found places advertised on the internet. However the homes we saw on the internet and those same ones that we went to look at were totally a joke. The pictures were not updated and we ended up seeing homes that had become fixer-uppers. We found broken down places. We both had been there, done that, and at sixty and sixty six years of age, neither of us wanted that.

I didn't understand why we couldn't build a home on our land, as I now was doing with three acres. Our home is in the heart of the Kettle Moraine Forest and it is so much like being up north. The view is awesome. Did I try to talk with him? Yes, over and over, I wanted to talk about what was so wrong. After all we had gone through in our years of marriage, I certainly didn't want things to end like this.

I wanted to go fishing, and to have vacations that we

never took in years gone by. I so encouraged him to retire because I could see how sick of work he was. I didn't take into consideration the change of retirement would bring devastation to my personal life. All the years of not drinking and here I was faced with a life changing decision. I just couldn't go back to the drinking days.

Alcoholism is ugly! The scripture tells us that Satan comes to rob, kill and destroy. That is one way he does it. He uses alcohol as we know. People are destroyed for lack of knowledge. This is a part of what I lived and struggled with. That old message that said "it's my fault" was played, but this time I knew in my heart it was a huge lie! I know that I was willing to listen to what he thought our problem was, but there wasn't anything I could say to get the communication started.

What was God's plan for me? Where would I live? What would I do with the animals? I know my heart was so totally broken. I wanted to give up! One evening as I lay in bed, I prayed that God would take me home. There just didn't seem to be any reason to go on.

> "For I know the plans I have for you", declares the LORD, "plans to prosper you and not harm you, plans to give you hope and a future."
> Jeremiah 29:11 (NIV)

Chapter 13

Parting and Reconciliation

Somehow, deep within my heart I knew my God walked with me despite my circumstances. Questions I had could only be answered by the Lord. In due time, I would come to understand more. In the meantime, I clung to my relationship with God and prayed continually for His wisdom and guidance.

Words seem inadequate as I try to describe how I feel about my family. My daughter Connie and her husband Michael own a beautiful horse ranch. Mike has a skid steer machine. Once my home was in place and the work of landscaping began, Connie became the designer of where and how the stones would be placed. Michael worked with his skid steer, moving and placing stones where Connie was asking him to place them. I had purchased huge stones for the base of the burms that would hold back the hill. It was beautiful to watch, like a picture puzzle. Connie did an awesome job! The stones were the pieces and each stone had to fit into the puzzle perfectly.

My entire family gave encouragement and help where ever they could. By God's grace the shattered pieces of our lives were brought back together. We were always in touch with one another during the time Jerry was up north. It was during that time that I told him via email about Joyce Meyer and her ministry on TV. Several days later, he wrote back saying, "She is good!" It took

God intervening many times. I came to appreciate as Jerry did also, The Joyce Meyer Ministry that Joyce and her husband Dave established. She is an excellent life and Bible teacher and both Jer and I watched the program in the mornings.

I know in my heart my husband had received Christ as his Savior many years earlier. I believed God did a work in his heart. He knew he belonged back home with us. I personally needed more than anything to surrender to the Lord and to forgive. This wouldn't be for the kid's sake or for Jerry's sake but it was for mine. Without Christ the process never would have started. It wasn't easy by any means. I knew that forgiveness was a choice and not a feeling however the feelings had to be dealt with. I had a lot of mixed feelings and anger was number one. I was angry with my husband that he left in the first place. I was angry that drinking had become an issue again. Hurt and anger filled my heart.

You have to understand something about me. Something that I feel I learned growing up, and in the early years of our marriage. Until I asked Jesus Christ to be my Lord and Savior, I kept grudges! There was a time in my life I regretfully admit, I could tell you to get lost rather than give you any kind of understanding or compassion.

I know I was like that because of the deep pain I carried in my heart. I didn't have time to hear about your struggles. I came to believe that being tough was the only way you were given respect and no one could hurt you. God knew and understood my pain and His Word now penetrated my heart. When I became willing to surrender, God walked beside me. No room for grudges. My prayer became,

> "Create in me a clean heart O God, and renew a right preserving, and steadfast spirit within me." Psalm 51:10 (NIV)

There were times when Jerry came down to help with the landscaping and we would talk. When the time was right, he gave me his commitment of not drinking, if he were to move back. The future would reveal to my heart how important forgiveness is. We both agreed for him to move back.

Chapter 14

Confronting the Big "C"

In April of 2003, I was diagnosed with breast cancer and the doctor thought we would be doing surgery and radiation. He told us I was estrogen dominant and that the cancer was a slow growing cancer. He told us he would be meeting with several other doctors and they would be going over the procedures they thought would be appropriate for their patients which included my case. I was numb! I couldn't believe that this horrible thing was upon me.

When you are faced with something as devastating as this news, I found there was really no where to run except to the arms of my Lord. I found myself asking, "Lord is this how my life will end?"

At first there was denial. This just couldn't be happening. It was as though all the challenges in my life up to this point were all washed away in the tears I now shed. I knew my life was totally in the hands of my Lord and I was scared and uncertain. In the days ahead I spent time in prayer. Seeking the Lord and asking Him to help me. Unless you have been in my shoes, you can't understand what it feels like to be handed a diagnosis that could possibly end your entire life. I became aware of how much more I wanted to live!

Our Pastor at that time asked everyone at our Saturday

service who wanted to stay after the service to do so. They would lay hands on me and pray for healing. Pastor Bill anointed me with oil and when all was said and done, I knew I needed the Lord's peace.

> "Is any one of you sick? He should call the elders of the church to pray over him and anoint him with oil in the name of the Lord." James 5:14 (NIV)

There were decisions to be made, and in the midst of the turmoil, I wanted to have the peace that surpasses all human understanding. When we met again with the doctors, he told us that I would need the surgery, a lumpectomy, followed by radiation. The days ahead were hard. I needed to trust that God knew what was best.

After the first surgery, the doctor told us that he felt I should have a second surgery. He wanted to make sure there were clean margins in the area where the cancer had been. It was agreed upon to have the second surgery. This of course took place over several weeks. I needed to trust my Lord and Savior totally. I was now at that place.

In the days that followed, it was suggested to me to talk with Dr. Michelle. She is a naturopathic doctor and I had great respect for her. I trusted her opinion and I called her. We talked for some time and I asked her what she would do if this was happening to her?

Based on the information I gave her about my cancer, she replied by telling me about a clinic that would treat my cancer without doing the radiation. I knew in my heart, this was the way I would walk. My journey began by going twice a week for IV's. They were filled with powerful vitamins that would knock out any cancerous cells that might be left behind after surgery.

Once again my life was filled with learning how to lean on my Lord. I had to learn to trust Him and not be filled with worry and frustration. I will never say those words lightly because it took surrendering my will, my life as I knew it, over to Him again and again. Sometimes moment by moment but I came to trust Him with the outcome. I had committed to having a mammogram yearly before cancer and I have followed this plan to this very day.

> "Trust in the Lord with all your heart and lean not on your own understanding: in all your ways acknowledge him, and He will make your paths straight. Do not be wise in your own eyes, fear the Lord and shun evil. This will bring health to your body and nourishment to your bones."
> Proverbs 3:5-8 (NIV)

Chapter 15

CJ Bey Kincade

*W*hen we purchased ET, I not only received a beautiful horse to love for all these years, but the Lord provided a new song in my heart. He has grown old with me and the love for him will always be in my heart along with so much gratitude. Once again the Lord brought healing where there was brokenness. ET and I have spent SO many wonderful rides together and he always gives me his best. My "Sudden Glory" boy!

I am so very proud of him. I thought at times I would have liked to show him in western pleasure classes. Our girls were becoming more involved in showing their horses so that became the center of my focus. I loved watching the girls on their horses and was continually on the rail, giving them encouragement. As of 2006 ET had been with me twenty four years and during those years he had developed health problems. I have struggled many times trying to find the answers for him to make his life better. Some things like acupuncture and prescription drugs the veterinarian prescribed helped but only for short periods.

Once again the Lord allowed me to receive knowledge about bare foot trimming. Changing how his feet were trimmed and changing his diet helped. His problems were on going and in 2004, he was doing really bad. I didn't know how much longer I could watch him struggle because he could barely walk. I began to question my motives. He is so special to the "little girl" inside of me and the love I felt for him and yet, I thought that I was being selfish in wanting to keep him alive.

I would pray continually, "Lord please help me. What am I to do? Is it our time to say goodbye?" It was about this time that my daughter Christine said to me, "Mom, why don't you think about getting another horse before you have to make that decision about ET?" At first the thought was repulsive to me! I found that even though I always want to do God's will for my life the thought of putting my wonderful horse to sleep broke my heart. I had simply rejected the thought of getting another horse.

In time however, I gradually found myself thinking more toward looking for a horse in the following year. This might be something that possibly could happen. For months I would go to the Arabian horse web page and look to see what was for sale. I looked for over six months. I went with my husband and Christine to see some of the horses that were close enough from our home. We had some really disappointing days!

I felt that as beautiful as ET was, none of the horses could hold a candle to him. I think I realized I was very prejudice and began thinking it was not meant to be. The Lord then reminded me to open my heart to his possibilities! I find as I walk with the Lord, He knows my heart, He knows my desires and I continually need to trust in Him.

If there is something that is in His will for my life, whatever the situation, He will bring it to pass. If it isn't His will, then He has something better in His plan for my life. It's really that simple. What is the biggest requirement that is needed? Trusting Him!

When I had gone on the computer and had looked at the Arabians available, I had looked at a picture of a gelding that was considered to be a black bay, instead of red, like that of my ET. This horse had white on one front foot and the opposite back hoof. When I first saw the picture, I really didn't care to learn more about the horse.

I believe the Lord brought my mind back to the picture of this horse several weeks later. Unlike all the other horses I saw, this horse was only one hour away from home instead of three or four so we decided to go and see him. Jerry, Christine and I again set out to look.

We stopped in our travels to eat lunch because we had some extra time before getting to the farm where this horse lived. Jerry and Christine were ahead of me in getting out of the vehicle as I was looking for something in my purse and they already had entered the restaurant. I had gotten out of the van, grabbed the sliding door to close it and pulled it with as much force as I could. Because it had started raining and the van door was wet I caught my index finger in the door. It slammed shut on it! I stood in terrible pain and was trying desperately to open the door with my right hand. When I finally released the door, I could see the blood on my hand and knew my finger nail had been hurt badly.

I went straight to the ladies room inside the restaurant. Christine came in saying, "Mom, what are you doing?" I proceeded to hold my finger up so she could see that it was bleeding quite badly. She asked if I was alright and I nodded yes, and with that she left only to come back with one of the men who was working in the kitchen who was an E.M.T. and he then offered me an ice pack. Oh how good that felt, as my finger and hand throbbed with pain. Needless to say this was not the best way to go and focus on a horse that might be a possibility for me but the pain didn't stop me, and I did want to see him. So we continued to the farm at which he was waiting.

As we stood and watched the young woman bring this horse out and proceed to tack him up, I kept asking the Lord to please confirm for me that this was or was not the horse for me. I again have to say that flashy he was not. I had been spoiled with ET'S beauty, white socks on his feet and star on the forehead.

The young woman, who owned him with her mom, shared my daughter's name, Christine. As we watched her with the gelding, her mom approached and Christine introduced us and said her name was Jeri. As I listened to her, I began to sense a quickening in my spirit. How could this be? Was this just a coincidence? When you believe as I do, they are called:

God Incidents

This mother and daughter had the exact names as my daughter and husband. What are the chances of this happening? I believe that God controls my life and all that happens in it. When I prayed to Him to help me to see His hand in this situation, I believed he was giving me His answer.

I began to feel an excitement within my heart. I just knew God was here in the now. About this time, I asked what the horses name was and Jeri replied, "Well, we didn't know what to call him, so we ended up giving him the name CJ." I was pretty excited by now, thinking how awesome is this?

My daughter Christine and my hubby Jerry are here with me looking at this horse named, CJ. At this point, we had walked into the indoor arena and as we stood looking at the open doors at the end of the barn we saw sheets of water pouring past the opening. It was storming outside and the thunder and noise of the rain coming down on the metal roof of the arena was terribly loud.

It felt like we were going to be blown away at any given moment. The young woman rode CJ through the entrance, began going around with him and despite all the clatter, rain and thunder, CJ behaved wonderfully and was a beauty to behold!

He was beautiful! It was something I will not forget. As I thought about whether or not we would purchase him, I continued to pray for God's will. Each step was very important to me. This gelding would have to come on a trial basis. He could not be mean to my old boy because ET deserved to live out his days in peace. He was the number one horse in my heart. Little did I know what God had planned for ET and myself.

The big day came! May 31, 2004. Once again a horse trailer pulled into my drive way and out walked CJ. We took him up to greet ET and they became friends almost immediately because he missed having another horse friend. They greeted one another as though they were old friends.

ET suffered from laminitis (which is inflammation of the lamiae covering the hoof), for several years now. I have looked for answers and have done so many things to make the quality of his life better. Prayer has literally enveloped my wanting to bring health to this wonderful horse and God knew the plea in my heart to do so. When CJ came to live with us, he brought healing to ET. He would go behind ET and literally push him with his front legs and chest, asking ET to move.

It was one of those moments when tears came to my eyes and gratitude flowed from my heart to my Father in heaven. CJ was gentle and took his time moving ET. The more CJ moved ET, the better ET became. Walking would cause flow of blood to the foot, and that's what he needed so badly. He wouldn't walk on his own, but given the encouragement that CJ gave, he did walk a lot more. It brought much healing and I laughed every time when I watched the two of them.

There were times when ET would lay his ears back at CJ, looking like he was telling CJ to buzz off! CJ just kept to the business at hand, gently move this old boy down the hill and into the pasture. The two of them slowly made their way down the hill with CJ walking behind ET.

About a month after purchasing CJ, we had our farrier come to do the trimming of the horses' feet. On this day, I shared with Tracy, the farrier who was also a Christian, my story. I told her how CJ came into my life and how it was a great adventure. How the names of my husband and daughter became a conformation for me. She listened to me telling her every bit of the details and most important, the fact that I truly came to understand in my heart of hearts that I did not want to buy CJ, if God had a different plan for me.

Experience is a good teacher if we will pay attention. I knew I needed to trust and obey, to then leave the consequences to my Lord. As I finished sharing, my farrier looked at me and said, "Nancy how awesome is that! His name is CJ, meaning Christ Jesus!"

My mouth came open and I stood in awe, not believing I had totally missed this! I believed God confirmed my purchasing CJ through the names Christine and Jerry, and that in itself was so very exciting!

I never made the connection that will continually remind me every day of my life, how much God loves me. I felt embarrassed, humbled and foolish all at the same time. How could I have missed this? I looked up to the heavens and with a child like faith; I could visualize my Lord Jesus looking down upon me. He was shaking his head from side to side saying *"My child don't you know how much I love you?"*

I had come to the place in my life, where I could honestly say to the Lord, if this is what you want for my life, then so be it. If it isn't right for my life then I don't want it. Do you have any idea, how hard that was for me, loving horses all of my life? I just couldn't imagine not having a horse. I believed the time for ET in his condition would not be long. However, I didn't want this horse unless I knew in my heart that he was right for me.

God had a divine purpose. I needed to walk the walk, one step at a time. God helped me to see that whenever I would call this horse's name, God would remind me *"I have been with you and I am still with you."* As a child looks to his or her parent for reassurance, I believe in my heart God wanted me to once again trust my Father in Heaven with all of my heart.

I was so humbled by the awesome way the Lord said *"I love you my child."* I believe as a child growing up I learned that asking for something of importance to me, just didn't seem to matter. I had stopped asking many years earlier. My human dad wasn't able to hear the cry of my heart when it came to having my own horse. This isn't to blame my dad anymore, but rather it is to help others to hear from my heart. Giving my life over to the care of God as I now know Him, has given me joy unspeakable. I can tell you He is who He says He is. He is the great "I AM".

The Lord made it obvious that his plan for ET and me was to bring CJ into our lives. CJ caused ET to keep moving and that in return caused good blood flow to his feet and that gave ET better health. He would continue to live a more healthy life for the next four years, none of which I would have had if it hadn't been for me getting this kind hearted horse CJ. ET actually became ride-able again.

God taught me many things by allowing me to have CJ.

On that special day in 2006, God placed into my heart and mind the thoughts of journaling my walk in life with Him. To share the years I've had a relationship with Him. I had asked this question. "Lord," I said, "What title would I give to my journal?" Almost immediately, "One Woman- One God- And a horse named CJ" came to my mind, and this would be the title. I was going downstairs at this time and I laughed out loud. I thought "CJ"?

"Lord," I said, "Why CJ?" I would think my boy of twenty five years would be the name My ET, not CJ. When I reached the bottom of the steps I turned and heard the Christian radio station. The host said the following, "If ever you are looking to publish something, just go to Christian Publishing.com."

I stopped dead in my tracks! I believed in my heart those words came from God. I needed to walk the walk one step at a time. I did start my journal, but never with the expectation of actually publishing it.

What I came to understand very simply was this. CJ gave ET all of what I have described and they were best buddies. CJ also became a testimony to my years of learning how to persevere when bad things happen in your life, such as falling off my CJ and cracking three ribs. It was my fault it happened. It was a rider error. In doing so, I lost all my confidence. I wasn't able to get on him and return to riding. My body needed to heal. That in itself broke my heart. I have been a horseback rider for fifty five years. I was now facing the possibility that my riding days were over. I became afraid and fear can destroy.

We know there is a healthy fear that is given to us by God and it often protects us. Fear also is something that can be a tool used by Satan against us. The end result would be to destroy us. I had become afraid to do something I had loved to do since I was fourteen-years-old. It took physical healing, and wanting to ride again, and the encouragement of others to overcome my fear, and get back on a horse. It didn't happen overnight but rather a lot longer than I wanted. It was in 2006 that I took my spill and it wasn't until 2008 that I started to ride a little.

Sometimes I would think to myself, maybe its time to stop riding all together. I am getting older and I sure don't want to fall off again. If I had been able to get back up that day and get on him, I know I would have made a quicker recovery. That wasn't the case however. I needed time for my body to heal and I went often to my chiropractor. The journey became longer than I wanted as I also fell on black ice during my time of healing. I thanked God for the heavy jacket I had on, but each time my body paid a price. I couldn't spring back the way I did when I was younger.

All of my determination came from the desire to continue to ride. Trail riding at a walk is all I ever did. The years of galloping or trotting through the woods no longer interested me. I simply enjoyed the peace and quiet and the joy I felt in being on my horse. My life was changing so quickly in the days ahead and many days would now come and go and I wouldn't be doing any riding. How do you hang on to something that you love so much and yet the obstacles in front of you are there and the losses you are about to endure are overwhelming.

I know in my heart that my faith in my Lord and Savior is what brought me this far. There is a little plaque that hangs in my bathroom and it reads as follows: PLEASE BE PATIENT WITH ME, GOD ISN'T FINISHED WITH ME AS YET! I just believed I would enjoy the gift of horseback riding a few more years with the help of my Lord. Little did I know what major changes my life held for me. The years from 2000 to 2008 were filled with so many unexpected changes.

Sometimes, it is so hard to comprehend how our lives can change so quickly. I had much more to learn about God's grace working in my life and the lives of my family and the creating of a life long tapestry. Bringing the reality of who Christ is and how to have a relationship with Him was something I wanted for each of my children. God has honored my prayers as a Mom so many times. At different times in their lives, I have shared with each of my kid's my love for our Lord and I know, it is their choice in life to ask Him to be their Lord and Savior and seek to have a relationship with Him.

Chapter 16

A New Role for My Life

As parents we hope to contribute to our children's lives by instilling good morals and values. We taught our children to be responsible, hard working people. We ate dinners together. We worked together as a family unit on different projects. We played together. These are some of the things that helped to knit us together as a family and create good values. You hope and pray that each of your children will be responsible adults someday. We both believed our children have grown up to be loving, hard working, caring people.

We had a lot of hard times and a lot of brokenness in our lives. We also failed our kids at times from being the parents they needed us to be. Hindsight is always twenty, twenty. Raising them in a Christ centered home, sharing God's Word with them and teaching them what it had for them at a young age wasn't accomplished in the way I would have liked.

We did have years that have created good memories. Jer was notorious for one liners: "Hold it in the furrow" "Whatever, whatever, whatever." When the grandchildren came to visit, he would say goodbye with "Happy Trails" "Thanks for the bonding" and when it came to horse back riding, quite often you would hear him say the famous "Tighter on the snaffle".

For a man who didn't talk a lot, he did have lasting one

liners most of which were funny to hear. At the horse shows he was the camera man. He would carry the big recorder to each show and tape the girls riding their horses. There are so many memories! I have decided to keep the good ones and let go of the bad ones and I truly believe that writing all of this has brought much healing. I didn't want anger, unforgiveness, resentments or the possible hardening of my heart to steal any more time from my life than what already was stolen over the years, before I met my Savior. There were lots of memories that brought me much laughter.

Was there pain? Yes, deeply felt in many areas of my life. In the years of retirement, when life and struggles should be less, at least in some ways, the children are all grown and on their own. And hopefully work hasn't become the main focus, I thought hobbies and vacations would now be enjoyed That was my dream, but not my reality.

In 2005, Jerry and I decided to build an addition onto our existing home. It would give us a larger living room with a gas fireplace that I would truly love. Jer and a carpenter we knew worked together creating a room of beauty and joy. We both loved wood and decided to do some of the walls and ceiling in cedar. We also decided to have sky lights in the room which made it a bright and warm room to relax in.

There were so many times I would stand in the doorway of our living room and tell him how beautiful the room was and how much I loved it. He had many talents. He enjoyed the work and by the time it was fully completed, we absolutely loved it.

In September of 2007, Jer wasn't feeling good and so we went to the doctor. He was diagnosed with lung cancer. We all were very saddened by this news. Jer received prayer, the laying of hands and anointment of oil from the elders of our church and Pastor Tom. We felt positive and looked to the Lord to bring healing. Of course we want the healing of our choice and that would have been to have Jer live much longer than he did. Each appointment at the clinic was very hard and Jody would be there to encourage her Dad and me. From September on we spent days going back and forth to the clinic. I know in my heart that God walked with us.

Then that horrible evening in February came. This awful thing was upon us and I didn't want it! I ran to get the phone and with trembling hands, I dialed 911. February 6, 2007 how do I write about this day? This day will change my life forever, because it is the day, angels carried my husband home to be with the Lord to live in heaven forever.

> "Absent from the body, present with the Lord!"
> II Cor 5:8 (KJ)

From this day forward, I walk in a new role in life; that of a widow.

I have heard it said, "Losing someone you love is like an amputation. That part of your life is gone and now you have to find out how to live without it."

On the day following my husband's death, something unexpected happened.

My daughters and I sat in the living room talking when the door bell rang. It was the mail man and he handed me a box that came from my friend Cathy in Florida. Normally I would have taken the package and set it on the table but because it was from Cathy something encouraged me to open the box.

Cathy didn't know at this point that Jerry had died the evening before. I took the box into the living room and opened it. It held a special coffee cup. Both Cathy and I love "Really

Wooley" art work from Dayspring, a Christian greeting card company. It had little baby lambs going all around the cup but the most important part of this cup was the scripture written on it. I am grateful to my wonderful friend for following what God had placed upon her heart.

> "We are God's workmanship, created in Christ Jesus to do good works, which God prepared in advance for us to do." Eph 2:10 (NIV)

The answer I had looked for, prayed for and had not received, came in Gods timing, not mine. I broke down crying when I read the scripture. The Lord had sent me a personal message to my heart. I knew right then He was speaking to me. Up to that point in my life, I always wondered if I was truly doing what the Lord wanted for me.

I knew that through all the rough times in my marriage I questioned whether it was God's will for me to remain in my marriage. There were times I asked the Lord to please answer me as to whether or not I should separate or get a divorce.

I cried out asking for an answer. It seemed to me His voice was silent. I never heard His answer until that day, in the scripture written on this beautiful cup.

When I talked with Cathy about this, thanking her for the cup, she told me she had bought it months earlier and kept thinking to herself that she needed to get it in the mail. Cathy and I have been neighbors and friends for a long time and we both have shared the love of the Shar-Pei. God has perfect timing, even when it was a painful, painful time.

How awesome is He! Just think how exact His timing was in all of this! If ever I believed in God's timing for something, this definitely was an unbelievable moment. I immediately felt as though our Lord had put His arms around my heart and He kept it from breaking into a trillion pieces. I will hold this memory in my heart forever. As I sit alone writing this, I realize just how many times God has encouraged me since Jerry's death with this Scripture written on my cup. I no longer doubt whether or not it was God's will for my life to stay in my marriage and I am so glad I sought the answer from my Lord.

In the weeks that followed my husband's death, a song was being played on the Christian radio stations. When I first heard it I cried so hard because the words tell you that we are being sung to by the person we have said, "goodbye" to for now. It was one of the ways God began to bring healing to my heart.

"Wish You Were Here" Mark Harris

Verse 1 -I wanted to tell you- How closely I've kept- The memories of you in my heart.
And all of the lifetimes –That we've had to share Live even though we're apart. Don't cry for me 'cause I'm finally free.

There are many ways the Holy Spirit ministered to me. He is the Comforter and the Healer. The words of this song told me my husband kept the memories of our lives (which meant the memories of our five children and myself in his heart.) He tells us not to cry for him *'cause he is finally free.* I was sitting with so many mixed feelings. I was happy for him but sad for us who are here missing him. I believed with all my heart the angels were with him and more than anything I believed he is worshipping our Lord! That is where he will be when I finally find him and then, I too shall be free!

It seemed like each time I would walk out to the barn in the morning and evenings to do my chores, I would end up just sitting quietly and listening with tears flowing down my cheeks. Sometimes I would hear the song from my radio inside of the barn as I came to the barn door. The words ministered to my heart and flooded my soul.

For weeks on end, I heard it play and it was like sweet honey to a very broken heart. I will never forget how many times I felt the warm presence of the Holy Spirit and the comfort He gave to me. God was there to hold me in His arms.

It was less than a month after my hubby's death that I received another blow. On March 5, 2007, my companion of eight years, "Ruthie" my beloved Shar-Pei and I said goodbye. When she died, it felt in my heart like another piece of me died. She truly was like a human. She understood things I taught her so quickly. She was the best. Wherever I was, she was also.

Devoted and loving. I felt like my world was crashing out from under me and there was no place to hide but into the arms of my Lord and Savior and I can tell you so honestly, I don't think I have never hurt this much. In the weeks that followed there were grief filled days that never seemed to end. I felt as though I were drowning. I cried out to Jesus!

Others who love you so much, family and close friends help to carry you through the pain. Being the kind of person I was, and still am, my little Shar-Pei are so very special. Each and every animal I have ever had the privilege of owning has brought to my heart the love given to me from my Father in Heaven. I believe God has used my animals to teach me so much about His unconditional love. Without them in my life, I really believe I would have become a victim of my circumstances and lived an angry life my entire life, filled with resentments and pain.

Ruthie made me smile so many times. She brought much laughter and joy. It was as though she knew what I was thinking before I thought it. She loved Jer so much and had to sit with him in the swing outside as they would do. He would say things like "What do you want wubby wips?" and she would get up on the swing next to him and sit as close to him as she could, wrapping his arm around her. In her eyes he was the best! They would sit together looking out across the Kettle Moraine Forrest. One day I got my camera and took a picture of them from the back. They were sitting on the swing, as I have described and I have it today next to me on the computer. Whenever I look at the picture, I just have to smile. It's so them.

CHAPTER 17

NEW LIFE

As the days and weeks went by my girls kept asking me if maybe I didn't want to look into getting a new puppy. Christine one day said, Mom I think you need to look into just that. I said no. I didn't feel I could afford it and I was so broken by the losses.

My grieving seemed to be carrying me in a huge downward spiral, into a pit of depression, a valley so deep. All of the things God had taught me in the past, I seemed to cling too, not knowing what the outcome was to be but wanting to trust my Father in Heaven.

> "The thief comes only in order to steal and kill and destroy. I came that they may have and enjoy life, and have it in abundance to the full, till it overflows." John 10:10 (AMP)

When you're at your weakest, that is when God can do so much! Joyce Meyer has referred to this scripture many times. It definitely has become a favorite of mine. I became aware of the spiritual warfare that was going on inside of me and I can't even begin to tell of the wonderful things my girls helped me with.

My entire family helped me in so many ways, wanting only the very best for me. It was obvious how they all were wanting and praying for the healing of my heart and body. Many times I just felt unworthy of their precious love. I realized more than once that they had a lot of healing also to go through and many times I wasn't able to help them as I would have liked to.

With lots of encouragement, I began wondering if getting a puppy would be a good thing. Again I asked the Lord for His will and if so would He please help me to find just the right pup and help me to be able to afford this precious new life.

And so it was, we prayed for His divine direction. Soon after, on a Saturday morning I was going to church for a meeting and before I was to leave I heard my water softener running and it wasn't at the correct time for it to soften the water. I called Chris and she told me to go ahead and she would come over and watch to see that all was working.

During the time she was downstairs she saw a basket with cards in it. Birthday cards and Father's day cards and then her attention was drawn to one special one. It was addressed to Jer and it was from Darren and Jody. When Chris looked inside there was a great surprise waiting for me. She left the card on the table with a note for me when I came home. It said "Mom before you look inside this card call me!"

So I did.

"Mom," Chris said," Now look inside the card." There inside was a hundred dollar bill. It was a thank you card from the kids, thanking Jer for putting in a laminate wood floor in their living room. Chris said, "Mom, Dad would want you to have this for a new puppy."

We both cried. Call me silly if you will, but I truly believe God cares that deeply about us and he knew that Jer probably meant to give that one hundred dollar bill back to his children but somehow forgot. He wasn't careless about money. The fact that it was still in the card, said to my heart that God knew it was there when the rest of us didn't. Jer helped me when it came to buying a new puppy. At one time he gave me three money envelopes and on the outside he wrote little notes. Each envelope contained a one hundred dollar bill.

On the first envelope the note read. "Thanks mom for all the good care you give to me when dad is gone to work. Love, Greta Rottweiler." The old bag, as he lovingly would call Greta who was getting on in age.

On the next one he said, "Thanks mom I appreciate the good care you give to me when Dad is at work. Love Ahna." Who was Greta's daughter.

And then the third envelope said, "Thanks mom for putting up with me when dad is gone to work. From, The Brat aka Emma." Emma was a puppy and full of herself most of the time.

He gave me that money when I was thinking about a pup, and that puppy turned out to be Jessie, Ruthie's mom. I knew in my heart that this one hundred dollar bill was a sign from the Lord that He was giving his stamp of approval towards the purchase of a new puppy. He had a precious puppy waiting for me to discover.

My church family sent me one hundred dollars toward her cost and my two precious friends, Bette & Cathy did the same. February 20, 2007 my sweetie was born. To have people care so much, is so very humbling. I am so blessed to have these people in my life.

Her name is Zoe, she is known as Zippen Zoe and she filled a hole in my heart. Once again, my journey in life has taken another turn, this time in the brightening direction. Bringing Zoe home on the second week of April with Christine and Jody by my side, definitely renewed my spirit and blessed me beyond words.

God's Healing Provision for a Broken Heart.
(Zippen) Zoe

Look, Mom, It's Snowing Out.

I still had Casey girl, Jer's last Rottweiler that we had gotten from a rescue. She was one year old on the day we picked her up and even though Jer and Casey didn't have a lot of years together, I know Casey loved him and he loved her. After losing Emma to cancer, He was still kind of depressed and didn't know if he wanted another dog.

He didn't want to make the investment of a puppy either. I knew he was sad about that so I went on line and looked at a Rottie Rescue and made contact. To my surprise they had just taken in this young dog. She already had been in three homes before she came to the rescue.

Casey was alone with me now and when the girls and I made a trip up north to get Zoe, Casey became so in love with her. She was an eighty pound Rottie and Zoe was an eight-week-old puppy. She was gentle with this Zoe and tried many times to be her Mama, bonding so closely. As I have said earlier, God has used my animals to teach me a lot of things in life.

Because Casey didn't have anyone to train her, she was like a bull in a china closet in many ways. I watched her closely as Zoe grew because I didn't want Casey hurting her accidently not realizing her body was so big and powerful. That's where Zoe got her additional name of Zippen Zoe. There were times when Casey was in hot pursuit of her. She would run as fast as she could and she would zip under the picnic table so Casey couldn't get her. It was pretty funny to see them. She would wait until the coast was clear or I had called Casey away from the table so she could escape.

Zoe was a snuggle bug as well and I loved that, especially at night. She would get up on the couch next to me, and still does to this day, snuggle up right next to me. She was my sweetheart and she knew it.

The days turned into weeks and the weeks into months. God does make provisions for us, and I have learned on a daily basis to turn my life over to him, to lean on Him, sometimes hourly.

November 30, 2007. This day had a special meaning to it. My day was starting out being very busy. Many things I felt needed to get done. After doing chores and taking care of my animals' needs and having breakfast myself, I bounced around from project to project. I took out the garbage, made out bills, washed dishes, worked on some little Christmas decorations, but not sticking to one thing until it was finished. Those moments are so hard on me. I feel so disjointed, like a butterfly fluttering back and forth trying to find that perfect flower to lie on.

Then, out of nowhere, I began to think about something Jer wanted for me last year at Christmas and because of his illness, I never did what he said for me to do. He had a bonus coming to him at one of the well known catalog stores. He would get catalogs through the mail all the time from this company and he had told me he had points coming to him, which meant one thing: money. I totally had forgotten. I knew he had point credits but didn't know the value and last year I wanted to get a new down coat.

I saw one in the book and said that it was really pretty to him. He thought so too and told me he had these points and I should go for it. I, on the other hand remember thinking I could make my jacket due another season and that he should be the one to spend the points for something he wanted.

Neither one of us did anything about this. Today, the Holy Spirit had to bring it to my attention several times for me to check it out. I called the company and told them that I was sure my husband had points accumulated but because he died this past February he never had the opportunity to use them and if I would be able to use them instead.

It took being connected to three different people before the answer was given. They were sorry for my loss and would give me Jer's points which would equal to seventy four dollars. They would send me a gift certificate for the amount and I can apply it to my beautiful down coat that I will receive as a Christmas present from my husband who is reigning in heaven.

The Holy Spirit has taught me so much. There is no stone left unturned by God, to those who choose to walk hand in hand with our Lord.

> "The Lord will open the heavens, the storehouse of His bounty to send rain on your land in due season and to bless all the work of your hands" Deuteronomy 28:12 (NIV)

There are so many ways He tells us how much he loves his children. Life brings with it brokenness, hardships, days that feel as though they will never end and yet God tells us again in His word that all that is required, is faith the size of a mustard seed. There have been times when I thought to myself, Lord it's all I have, a mustard seed of faith. There was more pain to go through. It just seemed there wasn't enough healing time for all that had come upon me. Grief is different for each person and no one can tell you to get over it. This is very personal. Having a relationship with God makes all the difference in the world.

October 20, 2008 became a day in which the Lord once again wrapped me in His arms of love. I had to say goodbye to my beloved riding companion of almost twenty six years. It was a lonely place to be at.

My ET, my little girl, dream come true horse. At the time we purchased ET, I felt my husband's support but now I had to make this decision alone. He truly was SUDDEN GLORY as his registered name indicates. He was a lovely gift from the Lord all those years past when my heart ached to have a childhood dream come true. As a child, no one seemed to hear, but the Lord did. He fulfilled the cry of my heart. The Lord helped me to open my heart again. My love for this animal became a healing ointment to my life.

Whether I was riding him, watching him out in the pasture, brushing his coat or standing beside him as the farrier trimmed his feet, I can honestly say I thanked God for this boy of mine, from the day I laid eyes on him at the State Fair to the day of laying him to rest.

The decision was very hard, and my wonderful daughters encouraged me and helped me the best they could. I truly missed my husband not being there, as I knew he loved ET also. I cried a bucket of tears. God giving me my ET, was such a big gift all those years ago.

There aren't words to describe the amount of joy I had in owning him and riding him and I believe with all my heart that you could have blind folded me and I would have trusted him to give me a wonderful ride. We had built a lot of trust between us over those years.

When I asked the Lord about the title of my journal and ET's name wasn't the first to come to mind, I was very taken back. God has since shown me that CJ became the means by which God would help me to remember always that He had given me my wonderful Sudden Glory. God brought CJ into my life. I now would have another four years with ET. The fact that CJ's name held my Savior's initials, Christ Jesus, was a forever reminder of who held my life in the palm of His hands.

One sweet memory I have about this painful time is this: My husband, as I have shared, was a man of few words. He had his one liners as we referred to them, and we would laugh and still do laugh about this. To think that his one liners would make such a difference to the people who loved him, I never thought about them in this way. But a few days after I put ET to sleep, I remembered that I had an appointment on the books with my farrier for the maintenance of ET's feet. I emailed him to cancel and he responded with kindness and as he signed his name, he wrote the words -"HAPPYTRAILS".

As I read these two words, tears flowed down my cheeks. Those were two words that Jer always spoke when someone went to leave our home, especially the grandchildren. Of all the words that could have been said, I personally believe our Lord touched my broken heart with these words and I felt at peace. I was taught to see the hand of our Lord in my life in every day and in every need, no matter how large or small we may think the need is. When I fear or struggle with anything, He has helped each and every time. He said in His word:

> "I will never leave thee, nor forsake thee."
> Josh 1:5(NIV)

The Lord was speaking to Joshua and told him, as He was with Moses, He would be with him also. I believe this applies to us as well. Our circumstances may be different, but His word remains the same. We have to remember He knows our hearts and God desires to bring healing to whatever area we are broken. It brings great comfort to my heart to remember these words.

In the pictures on the following page, you will see a woman and her horse. Not just any horse! These pictures describe my story about CJ in a special way. He has become quite the comedian. I just love this boy so much!

"A True Love Story"

"CJ look at this flower."

"No...No you can't eat it!!"

"Oh yes I can! Smile for the camera Mom!"

Chapter 18

Reaching Out in Song

I have decided to write about something that is precious to my heart. It is one of those things that came to me, totally unexpected. In 2008, my daughter Jody gave me the gift of having my one and only album put on CDs. The album originally was produced in 1981 and I surely never expected to be able to have it today.

There were times in my life when I struggled to believe in myself as a singer or to be able to share these songs on a record and have them be a blessing in someone else's life. The Holy Spirit gave me the opportunity to bless others and to bring joy and healing for them. I have always had a deep desire to help people understand how they, like me, can come into a wonderful relationship with our Father in Heaven.

When I received the CDs from Jody, I cried in awe of God's faithfulness to me. He has blessed people through the words when it had become an album and now I had CDs to continue the possibility of blessing another life! How awesome! My youngest daughter was being faithful to what God had put upon her heart. Bless her Lord Jesus!

Today He is doing the same, helping people to give the worries they have, over to Him. The first couple I shared my CD with was friends who lived quite close to me. They are retired as I am and like all of us, they were having some struggles which we shared with one another. I believe God gave me a nudge that day to share my CD with them.

I did just that! At a later time, she called and said to me, "Thank you so much Nancy! You will never know how much we listen to the songs over and over. It helped us so much!" My heart overflowed with joy and praise for my Savior and Lord. I believe Grace for my life was and still is underserved favor.

Chapter 19

Faith and "Wubby Wips"

Life brings so many challenges. Do we continue to walk with God through them or do we walk in our own strength? Reflecting on the years of my life has made me realize so many things. Even though the people in my life are so wonderful and very supportive, it is the daily conversations I have with my Lord that carry me into the later years of my journey here on earth.

Walking with the Lord is more important every day the longer He grants me life. In my own eyes, I don't feel like I have done anything great as the world would view being great. I've gone through some pretty rough years. I do so thank God for the comforting ways He works in my life because he always brings me to the place of the cross.

In 2009, it was suggested to me by two friends who were interested in new puppies for their lives, that if ever I again would have a litter of Shar-Pei they would be there for me in their commitment to a new puppy. I thought about this long and hard. I decided to seek the Lord. As I sought an answer from God these words seemed to stand out on the page in my Bible:

> "Only hold true to those things which you have already attained and walk and order your lives by that." Phil 3:16 (Amp)

I needed to walk one step at a time. I believe God was telling me that I had in the past attained Shar-Pei puppies from a certain stud dog I was now thinking about. I didn't consider myself a breeder that had litters of puppies very often. I had a total of seven litters including this one over a period of twenty five years while being part of this awesome breed.

My concern was whether or not I was up for the task. As always, the love I had for my friends who wanted a new baby and the love I had for Shar-Pei puppies weighed in as a positive. Life is a process of growing and wisdom is learning to make choices that you later won't regret. This whole process from day one required a huge commitment on my part.

To begin with we only had a fifty percent chance of having a pregnancy! We were using the stored semen from a male that I had used twice when he was alive. Cookie and Suzie which I already have shared about were his daughters. These were my beloved girls from years before and I felt influenced by the love I had for them.

The male had been gone over fourteen years. In the beginning of this adventure, I didn't know the owner of the male had stored semen. I had simply called her to ask if she knew of anyone in our area who was a good breeder. Neither one of us were active in showing or breeding. That is when I found out she had stored semen from her male.

This wasn't a simple decision for me as we would be doing an implantation of this semen. It all could have overwhelmed me. I never stopped praying or asking for God to be with me. Again I need to say, I didn't want to do this if it wasn't in God's will for my life. Was this the right decision? I am so grateful God doesn't let go of us and I tried with all my heart to do what I believed was from Him.

I had no regrets in producing one more litter of Chinese

Shar-Pei in my lifetime. We moved ahead and the time came when we did an ultra sound revealing a possible five puppies. I was in awe! I remember as I drove away from the veterinarian's office, tears welling up. Cathy had gone with me and we couldn't believe a possible five puppies were there. I was so excited and I couldn't wait to tell my family and call Bette and Jean!

We waited patiently and when the day came and these little bundles of Joy were born, I was a very nervous Mom. I was excited and somewhat apprehensive because it was a lot of years since I had a litter born and I didn't consider myself a spring chicken any more. Never fear when Jody and Christine are near! Chris and Jody both worked as veterinarian technicians for years. Both girls came and helped so beautifully in bringing forth new life.

It's so wonderful to witness one of the greatest gifts God has given to man. Here we were with five new lives! Joy unspeakable! The days were so full and I was so busy with these new babies. When they were about eight weeks old, they were going to their new home. Little Hannah and Gracie went to live with Jean and John.

Jean and I go back many years and she still has Mr. Gus from my Jessie's litter. He is ten-years-old now. That's how long it has been since my last litter. In talking with Jean, she describes Gracie as "the wiggler". Forever wagging her tail as she curves her body in a "U" shape. It's like she can't show you enough how happy she is. She also has her own special way of getting up on something without just jumping up on it. It just has to be seen!

Gracie is slender, dainty, and feminine. Hannah acts like a little tomboy. She is like a sumo wrestler. She is the adventurer. There isn't a dirt mound high enough that she wouldn't climb. She likes getting dirty and to be rough and loves to chase the cats! She also perches on the top of the couch so she can have a three hundred and sixty degree view of anything that moves in the room and at any given moment she can jump off her perch and begin her chase.

Gracie eats slowly, chews her food and is very clean. Hannah devours her food in seconds, leaves a huge mess and has slime hanging off her face. These two girls are the best sisters and best friends. They never fight over toys, food, walks or treats. They have so much respect for one another and give each other their space. I am so blessed to have them.

2009 MIRACLE LITTER

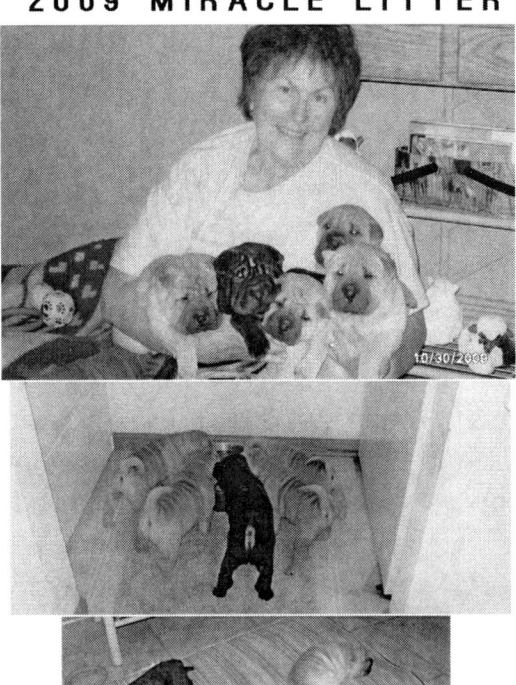

Chancey lives with Bette and Dale. Bette and I have been friends, what seems like forever. This is her second puppy from me over so many years ago. They drove up from Texas to pick their new baby up. Bette just wanted a Shar-Pei puppy (and I quote her), "I don't care if it's black, pink or purple. I just want a Glorybound Shar-Pei puppy!"

I asked Bette why they named her Chancey. As they drove back to Texas, they began talking about a name. They talked about different ones to give her but none seemed to be the perfect one. They had picked the name Sage and for the most part thought that's what they would give her.

However, they began talking about the fact that this was a beautiful miracle. We only had a fifty percent chance of having pups. To have five babies was awesome and out of this discussion Dale and Bette decided on the name Chancey. When Bette and I talk on the phone about this little honey of a puppy she will tell me things about her and whenever she would tell me this: "Chancey has her naughty pants on today", I would just laugh so hard! Bette and I both end up laughing over these silly dogs and all the joy they bring to us.

PUPPY LOVE

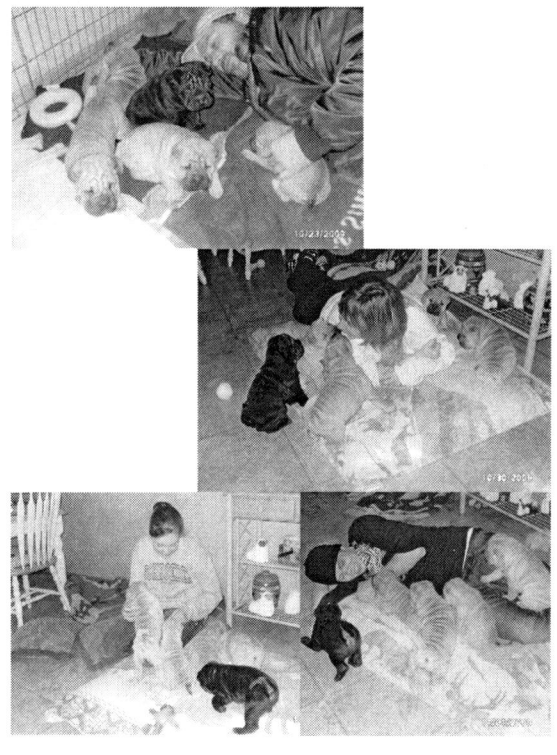

I didn't plan to keep two of the five; however I wouldn't change that now for anything. My male pup, I named Eli because he would stand over his sisters or be on the top of the pile when they were all playing. He would make us laugh so hard. When my son-in-law Tom would come over and lay on the floor and let the puppies come and kiss him or chew face, it was Eli, who would climb on top of Tom's back and sit as if he had conquered his opponent.

When the grandkids came we laughed often and with Jody and John it was the same. If anyone of them laid on the floor, they became fair game for all five pups to pile on. When I searched for a name on the computer, Eli, meaning "The Highest" was a natural.

I laugh so hard because he lives up to that name to this day. He is quick to learn and loves me so very much! His little sister, who after she was born became a concern for me, seemed so very tiny in the beginning. In my concern I was faced with the possibility of having to tube feed her. This was something I never experienced doing before. As always there is risk with a procedure and I was asking the Lord to please help me and to give me the courage if I had to do this. My veterinarian had said I would know when and if I would need to. He sent along the equipment to do so.

My prayer became "Help me Lord "so if I need to do this I would do it correctly, otherwise she could suffer and possibly die. Needless to say I watched her very closely to make sure the bigger pups like her brother wouldn't take all the milk.

I prayed and asked God to guide me. One evening I was sitting in the kitchen and had come up with the idea to take her apart from the other pups and let her nurse all she wanted on her own away from the pack several times extra in a day. As I sat watching her, she was facing me, lying on her tummy, nursing on momma dog. I could watch her closely.

Her lips were tightly closed on one of the nipples and she was drinking very intently when all of a sudden she opened her eyes and looked up into mine as I was bent over watching. Our eyes met and as little as she was, her little tail started wagging back and forth super fast. My heart just melted. You could tell she was a happy camper! It was as though she were telling me "thanks mom!" I said to her, "Oh my honey, this is what I need to do for you. Give you your own private fountain, to fill that tummy more often." I said out loud, "Thank you Jesus". I told her then that she would not be going anywhere that she was going to be my little Honey Bee.

To this day she is just that, sweet as honey and yet very capable of handling her big brother who is a lot bigger and stronger. We need to remember a honey bee is tiny but their sting is not! Eli has brought the joy of having a playmate for Zoe.

Zoe was always so much smaller than Cassie, so she never really had a playmate. She does now! I laugh so often over their antics together. The Shar-Pei are in my blood! Honey was the smallest in the litter but she has the biggest snore!

> "A happy heart makes the face cheerful, but heartache crushes the spirit."
> Proverbs 15:13 (NIV)

Today I sit at the computer and smile. "I'm not where I want to be, but thank God I'm not where I used to be." This is one of Joyce's sayings and boy it sure does fit! I have found peace now with myself and with my Lord. God has set me free! I have come to realize once again that you can't control what others do in their lives. The only life I am responsible for is my own. I now can look back at situations and see that my heart was grieved many times by things I had no control over.

Sometimes that feels really sad. I ask the Lord to search my heart and to show me if I have done anything to be ashamed of. I am not afraid to ask Him. I know if it is something that I need to look at, He will show me and it is up to me to change whatever needs to be changed through the power of the Holy Spirit. Years ago, I learned something that has helped me to look at myself and be honest. It is another one of those precious sayings that has been with me for along time.

> *"If I always do, what I have always done, then I will always get what I've always gotten."*

I know when I don't have peace in any situation I need to seek Him in His word or in prayer or just sitting and talking to the Holy Spirit. Maybe just sitting quietly and listening for Him to speak to my heart. The Holy Spirit is a person of the trinity, and He came to be our helper, our comforter and our healer.

We need to remember that Jesus said He was going away, but that He would send one much greater than himself to be there for us. Sometimes I just sit in the quiet. I will ask him about things that I have been praying about. I will talk to Him and then I will listen. With pen and paper, I write down what I think in my heart He is saying.

Way back in the 1980's I came to believe this. It has helped me understand my God a lot more. I need to keep my heart and mind open to Him. I have wanted from the first day I asked Christ into my life, to be my Lord and Savior, to never do anything displeasing to Him. I know I fail because I am human, but God's grace is always there to pick me back up.

> "Do not grieve; The joy of the Lord is your strength." Nehemiah 8:10 (NIV)

Once again as I strive to regain my confidence in doing something I love to do, I need to trust in God with all my heart! Horseback riding has meant a lot to me. It has always been a special time with God. My therapy time! Can I honestly let go of the "what if's?" All of the doubts and fears?

> "For I am the Lord your God, who takes hold
> of your right hand and says to you, Do not
> fear: I will help you." Isaiah 41:13 (NIV)

I began to look at all the things that had happened up to this point in time: I had fallen off my horse, cracked three ribs and no longer was able to ride a horse because of the pain. I again fell on black ice and reinjured myself and left me in much despair.

When the time came and I could ride, I discovered how fearful I was. This broke my heart! Knowing I had lost all the confidence I once had. I can't describe how that felt to me. I also had to acknowledge the fact that I didn't have the love for CJ that I once had for ET. Basically that was because I never really took the time to bond to him and I now realized this.

The years between the time of purchase in 2004-2007 were filled with major losses, my husband's death and the death of my best four legged buddy, Ruthie. Losing the confidence of horse back riding was still another blow! It seemed to me I sat in a pit of grief and depression. Praying and being in God's word helped me to search my heart and find answers. As my body healed, along with my broken heart, things became clear to me. I learned to look at the word, fear, in this way:

False **E**vidence **A**ppearing **R**eal. Wow! I liked that very much! The fear that I was experiencing was not godly fear. I began to understand that I needed to spend quality time with my boy. Not only did I brush him and groom him, I taught him how to give a hug. As I stood next to him, I would ask him to hug me. This meant for him to bring his head and neck around me as far as he could and I would take his head which he then would lay almost flat in my hands and I would give him a kiss next to his eye.

I know this probably sounds silly but as he learned how to do it, I began to fall in love with this sweet boy. When I would come out to feed him, he would call to me, not just once but he carried on a whole conversation.

I would call him "Mr.Ed". Remember the talking horse show on TV? He caused me to laugh so often and that brought more healing. If he was down in the pasture at dinner time I would call to him and he would come cantering up the hill to where I was. He was becoming my companion and good friend and I was falling in love with him so! I knew then I was on the right path.

> Courage is not the absence of fear.
> Courage is the presence of faith!

I began to ride him some on the barn lot. I was unsure of myself but determined too overcome this huge obstacle. I felt safe and secure on the barn lot. It took real courage to be willing to ride him out on the trails and for some time I just couldn't get up the confidence I needed.

My daughter, Chris helped to teach me the "calm down cue" and how to "disengage his hip" which CJ had been taught. He was taught to carry his head lower and I could cue him to do so and I learned how to ride with one hand on the buckle and the other on one rein.

This was for safety. It's a great thing to know because if the horse would bolt forward causing you to lose control, you then would have the ability to take hold of the one rein and pull his head to the side and slow him down. It was like having a hand brake rather than pulling on both reins.

It is a maneuver that I practice until it hopefully becomes second nature to me. That was the key, practicing this and having it be part of my knowledge and using it as a tool if I needed to. It just added to bringing my confidence level up. After riding in a certain manner so many years, the saying "You can't teach an old dog new tricks" seemed to be a reality for me for a time. I kept the faith that gave me courage and took the new knowledge and applied it to both myself and my CJ. I overcame the scared feelings of wanting to "give it all up."

I believe with all my heart because CJ was carrying the initials CJ, which in my heart stood for CHRIST JESUS. I was reminded all the time that He was a gift from my Lord. This was not the time to give up. I believe that if his name had not been what it is, at my age, I would have made the decision that I was contemplating. I would have lost the joy and peace and the accomplishment that was so long in coming.

This may not seem like much to someone else, but to me it has been life changing. Thank you, Lord, for never giving up on me, even when I am ready to give up on myself.

God allowed certain things to happen that changed the way I thought. Part of me thought that I needed to find a different horse for myself. I had looked for another horse, and in doing so came across a sweet gelding that was smaller than CJ in height. However, I needed to trust and believe with my heart that God has only the best waiting for us and even though sometimes we stumble, He is there picking us up.

What happened with this horse now affectionately known as "Charlie" is amazing to me. This little boy wasn't meant for me, but rather for my daughter Jody. God spoke to my heart at this crucial time. I couldn't give up on CJ or my ability to ride him. Instead, Jody fell in love with what she saw when we had gone to see Charlie.

I didn't know that Jody had told Chris, if I didn't buy him she thought she would like to. As God would have it, and not what Nancy thought she wanted to have, the Lord brought Charlie to live with CJ at my home. Jody now had a horse of her own. How very wonderful!

So many times in my life God has encouraged me to take small steps forward, filled with determination, and always doing that which I believe God wants for me. I know today, He wants me to know the joy and peace that comes from walking daily with Him. It was so nice to finally join my daughters, Jody and Christine on the trails again. We have laughed together so hard while we just walked our horses on the beautiful Kettle Moraine trails.

Organizing schedules together is always the challenge. I believe this is just another new beginning in my life and trusting God is what brought it thus far. Oh how I praise my Savior! To top it all off, my grandson Collin, gave me the opportunity to have him take pictures of myself and CJ. He snapped picture after picture of the two of us in different poses.

Now some of those very pictures are in beautiful frames on my living room wall. I know it may sound silly but, in the evening when I sit in my living room, I look at all of the pictures and I truly do give thanks for not only what I see in the pictures but for my loving family. Collin took the cover pictures for this book. What an awesome job!

There is another person who gave me an awesome gift and it was my daughter Cindy. She put together two picture albums. The first one is of me growing up, with pictures of me and my animals and also a wedding picture album which I never had until now. She is so talented and I cherish them both! You can look at them and see the hours of work she put into them, but more than that I see the LOVE.

Today I am a different person and I believe with my whole heart I needed God's power to break free of the past that was negative and to stay true to what God has planned for my life now. Prayer and God's mighty word are the tools used against any strongholds.

Opening my mind and heart to God and asking Him for the help I needed enabled me to change my way of thinking.

I continue each day to grow in His wisdom and strength.

We must always remember that on the other side of the tests we go through, there is promotion and there are rewards according to God's Word.

Remembering always that
JESUS IS LORD AND KING

To my Pastor Tom and Marianne, thank you! Your support has meant so much! You are loving, kind people and I thank you for being in my life. To all of my friends over the years, "Thank You!" To my beautiful daughters, my son and my son-in laws, my wonderful grandkids and great grand kids, I hope and pray that this book will be a blessing and encouragement to ALL of you. I pray that each of you will grow from it spiritually. Without God being who He is in my life there wouldn't be the wonderful lessons I have learned over the years of walking with him.

My prayer for each of you is that you will allow God to continually work in your life. His word is precious and true. As we walk through life we are challenged in so many ways and I found as I have stumbled, God has been there over and over to encourage my heart helping me to continually hear His voice above all others.

Words can never really describe the joy I feel in my heart now that I am back riding my CJ. Some struggles take longer than others. I believe the most important thing to remember is to keep your heart open to God. His word tells us over and over how He will walk with us.

> "Whatever you have learned or received or heard from me, or seen in me—put it into practice. And the God of peace will be with you." Phil 4:9 (NIV)

I thank God for the courage He gave me and the lesson of walking with him one step at a time, one day at a time. As I come to the finish line of writing, I want to share something that is dear to my heart!

One of the most important parts of this journal is the knowledge that without my husband there wouldn't be this journey of our life together, and although we both made mistakes, our Lord blessed our love and life together in so many ways.

There were five beautiful reasons born to us! I choose to believe they have the very best of the two of us living within each of them. Thank you Lord for all forty eight years Jerry and I had as husband and wife.

Our Grandkids

GRANDKIDS

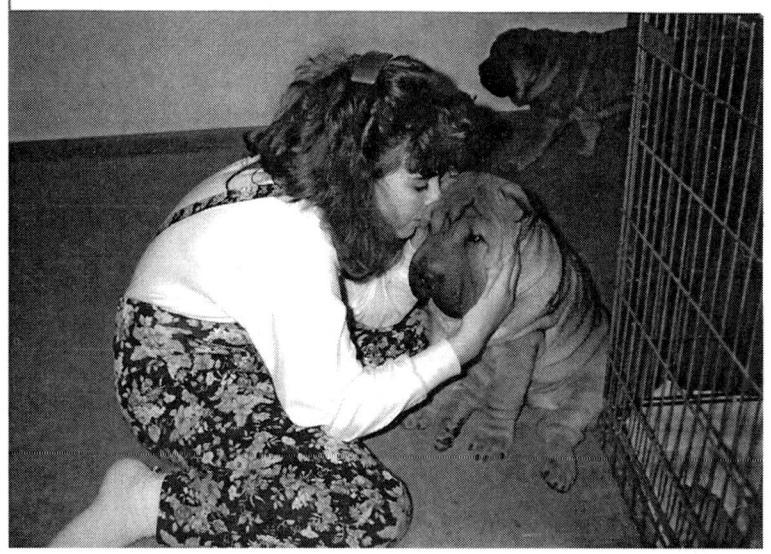

MORE GRANDKIDS

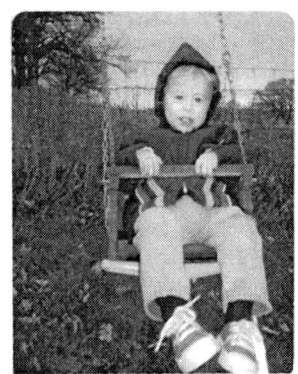

GREAT GRANDKIDS

CHAPTER 20

ONE MORE SPECIAL STORY

(One that is very special to my heart)

Jer wasn't a man of many words as I have said earlier. However he tried to make up for what he wasn't able to bring to the relationship. One way he did this was to give back to me something that I had lost in the early years of our marriage. It broke my heart back then and he knew it but financially wasn't able to change it.

On our eighteen wedding anniversary Jer gave to me a diamond ring. This ring will be worn by me until I come home to be with you, Lord. You see, back when I was pregnant with our son, I had gone swimming at my parent's home on the lake.

My fingers were swollen, so days earlier I had placed my original gold wedding band on my small finger. It fit perfectly. To my horror as I went into the water and my hand became submerged. Under the cold water my ring suddenly came off. I panicked, trying desperately to find it. I searched and searched and searched trying hard to not cry because I knew I wouldn't be able to see it. The ring went to a watery grave down in the sand below. It broke my heart and I had a very hard time accepting it was gone.

This diamond ring I wear today, that Jer gave to me, is so much more than just a store bought ring. He wanted me to have a half carat diamond. So we went to see a friend Jim, who was a gold smithy and made beautiful rings. We stopped over at his shop and we began to design what I thought I would like to have. I wanted the ring to look like two rings in one. It would represent both an engagement ring and a wedding ring. With Jim's help we drew a picture of what it might look like. I also decided that I wanted my mom's diamond from her wedding ring in it. Then we decided to use the gold that was in our two class rings also Jer had received a pin, every five years from his employer, each pin had a diamond in it.

Yep! These also had to be put in and around the larger diamonds. It was beautiful. Joy unspeakable! When we went to pick the ring up, I can't begin to tell you how the tears flowed.

It was such an awesome gift! Jim had created *a beautiful, one of a kind ring.* It had everything on it, even an engraved line that made it look like two rings in one. It meant so much to me, more than words can ever express and more healing came to both of our hearts. These are the kinds of things love is built with. God knew what was in both of our hearts and I believe our love for one another was manifested in the symbol of this ring.

As I have said in the beginning of this great and wonderful journey. It really all started with me searching for God and finding Him. We can never change ourselves in the beautiful way God will change our needs and wants through the relationship we build with Him. It has taken many seasons for me to come into the peace I have today.

"You are my hiding place: You will protect me from trouble and surround me with songs of deliverance." Psalm 32:7 (NIV)

Truly Lord Jesus, you did make a beautiful tapestry out of the brokenness we each carried into our marriage. My heart overflows with love. "HAPPY TRAILS" brings a special meaning to all of our hearts, along with the picture on the back cover. I just couldn't find a better way to say it!

Thanks JB.

(From left to right) Bottom row: Nancy, Jerry
Middle row: Christine, Jody, Cindy
Back row: John, Connie

A NOTE FROM THE AUTHOR:

This is an open invitation from me to anyone who has never confessed the Lord Jesus Christ as their Savior. I am asking you to take a moment to invite him into your heart, to confess your sins and ask for forgiveness. I know I talked about how and what I experienced in my life. Now I want to invite you to do the same. You will receive eternal life at the time of your death. God will bring blessings into your life now that you never would expect to receive! You can grow in the relationship you will now have with God.

He is who He says He is.

Trust the God of all creation, the God who wants nothing more than to welcome you into his loving arms. He is the God who gave His life for you, so that you could be with Him forever.

HAPPY TRAILS TO YOU UNTIL WE MEET AGAIN

CPSIA information can be obtained at www.ICGtesting.com
Printed in the USA
LVOW13s1738200713

343778LV00005B/12/P